A THREE-DIMENSIONAL
MODEL OF HUMAN BEHAVIOR

By

Michael Pak, M.D.

ISBN: 1-4033-4075-7 (e-book)
ISBN: 1-4033-4076-5 (Paperback)
ISBN: 1-4033-4077-3 (Dust Jacket)

This book is printed on acid free paper.

1stBooks – rev. 01/08/04

Printed in the United States of America

For information or to order additional books, please write:
1stBooks Publishing Co., Inc.
1663 Liberty Drive
Bloomington, IN 47403
U.S.A.
1-800-839-8640
Or visit our web site and on-line catalog at
www.1stbooks.com

For additional information about the
Three-Dimensional System of Behavior Analysis,
see U.S. Patent 6581037 at www.uspto.gov

CONTENTS

INTRODUCTION

HAVING LIVED IN SEVERAL DIFFERENT REGIONS OF THE WORLD, including Eastern and Western Europe, the West Coast of United States, and Middle America, I have observed some remarkably similar behavior patterns across societies. In particular, various negative behaviors, such as verbal threats and physical violence, appear to be expressed more freely and more lightly in certain cultures compared to others. These cultures also tend to assign a greater positive meaning to polite language and cooperation.

As some attending physicians in a Midwestern hospital argued with each other and the staff, I was perplexed by the general absence of concern and hostile emotions around such communication. The scenes looked almost like some staged antics and conflicts on television or in the theatre, but not quite. This conduct was serious, but it carried a very light negative meaning. While people didn't smile or communicate much, they still worked together reasonably well. Establishing good relationships required only a rudimentary level of positive communication such as brief eye contact, a smile, or a compliment—behaviors which elsewhere carried no particular positive meaning. The population apparently played by an entirely different set of rules than the ones I was used to in California. Variations, however, were not random—far from it. The trend was virtually identical to the one present across Europe. Did a fundamental principle connect these seemingly unrelated behaviors?

The answer to these and many other interesting observations came in the form of a three-dimensional model. I gradually realized that interactive behavior is a linear phenomenon guided by culturally-determined perceptions. Our actions range from very cooperative to very antagonistic along a more or less straight line, depending on how we interpret other people and feel toward them. This line of perception and action often becomes shifted so that we interpret and behave very differently under the same circumstances. A closely related trend in our interactions is their frequent tendency to become indirect and covert. The whole system of perception, action, and indirect or covert conduct can be plotted along X, Y, and Z axes to produce a three-dimensional model that can be used to understand, analyze, and to some degree even predict behavior.

The beauty of the three-dimensional model is its ability to integrate a great deal of information about people's thought process and actions, which can make certain trends clear to wide segments of the public as well as behavioral scientists. The system provides more than an intriguing subject for academic discussion. It has very real significance in daily lives and interactions among a majority of us, ranging from schoolchildren to the elderly and most everyone in between.

The stories presented here can serve as a template which explains the model. With this knowledge, readers' insights into cultures and people around them will hopefully grow in a positive direction, the same way my own have and continue to do so.

A detailed explanation of this model can be found in the summary on page 91, or online at www.uspto.gov (patent 6581037). Those who prefer a more gradual approach may wish to proceed straight to the chapters.

THE VISIT

FRANK, A FOURTEEN-YEAR-OLD FROM CONTINENTAL PLAINS, WAS passing a vacation with relatives near the coast on a trip filled with fun and excitement. He enjoyed seeing an older cousin who knew his way around and had breath-taking stories any fourteen-year-old would love to repeat to his friends back home. His relatives lived in a quiet, affluent neighborhood amid a row of old, but well-preserved, ivy-laden houses. During morning excursions around town and long summer afternoons spent in the front yard, he had a chance to meet with neighbors and introduce himself to young people in the area.

Early in the visit, Frank was invited to play in a soccer match with kids from nearby homes. He was more adept at basketball but felt he could easily hold his own against the native boys in any athletic competition. After usual introductions, the game started uneventfully. For the most part, play was reserved. Frank excelled and got his way throughout this contest. He displayed superior skill and strength. During the first period, a quick pass allowed him to make a particularly strong goal kick, which bounced off the goalie before it hit the net. The whole episode was pretty amusing.

"I told the guy to try using his hands next time," he would later recount.

Local players were docile and their level of tolerance was actually surprising. They made little or no attempt to push back, even when provoked. It seemed that players could get away with a few fouls without being yelled at or hit, let alone ejected from the game, the way they would be back home.

The second period went at a slower pace as both sides tired. After a goal from the other side, the game ended in a draw and his older cousin picked him up. For a change, Frank could impress his relative with a description of his feats during the match.

Although no further soccer took place in the following weeks, excitement continued as each out-of-town excursion brought a new experience. The uncle was an avid sailor who liked to spend free time at the harbor, an hour's drive from home. He owned a sailboat and took his nephew and sons for a weekend cruise. At sunrise, they navigated through a narrow channel and out to the open sea, passing a myriad of various-sized vessels along the way. For Frank, it was a brand new, unforgettable event. Their glide proceeded comfortably at eight knots with a favorable westward breeze. By midday, the wind and sea had strengthened, and men on deck were soaked. Still, sailing on a bright day through foamy crests was exhilarating.

When the sun disappeared behind a bank of clouds, it was time to head back. With the sails down, they motored toward the harbor against a brisk headwind. Frank and a younger cousin found comfort in the cabins below. A thunderstorm arrived and remaining time was spent in a hotel playing cards.

The next day, some friends joined them for a shopping trip and a walk along the beach. Frank saw a girl who had been introduced to him several days earlier. She approached, smiled, and greeted him warmly. She was tall, slightly older, and attractive, with long, straight brown hair. Frank was certainly interested, although her openly suggestive advance in public seemed strange.

"She must be quite promiscuous," he thought. He sent back a look of approval and then turned to rejoin his group.

He looked for the girl during the next few days, but she did not show up again, much to his disappointment.

Remainder of his vacation passed mostly uneventfully at seaside and around the house, except for one last incident that would become etched in the visitor's memory. Prior to departure, a confrontation occurred on the beach, which involved a local adolescent large for his age and fairly rigid. The attack came suddenly. Punched were thrown, and both kids had bloody faces before others intervened. Local individual came out better, but to the visitor, the outcome really wasn't as important as why this episode had happened in the first place. Upon examination of events, it turned out the only reason for the attack was Frank's failure to respond to a greeting.

"I said 'Hello' to that jerk, and he just walked past me without even looking my way," the kid accused, which Frank thought was an irrational action. With attentions focused elsewhere, he had hardly noticed the salutation. Besides, he wasn't in the habit of responding and certainly felt no obligation to do so.

I am not this guy's servant! He thought.

It was a sour note of an otherwise excellent vacation. For the most part, he would remember this visit with fondness and feel admiration for his older cousin and other relatives. He would often contemplate a move to that part of the world in the future to search for a better, more exciting life.

TO GAIN A MORE CLEAR UNDERSTANDING OF EVENTS DURING THE vacation, we need to grasp some concepts that form the basis of the three-dimensional model, illustrated in Figure1.

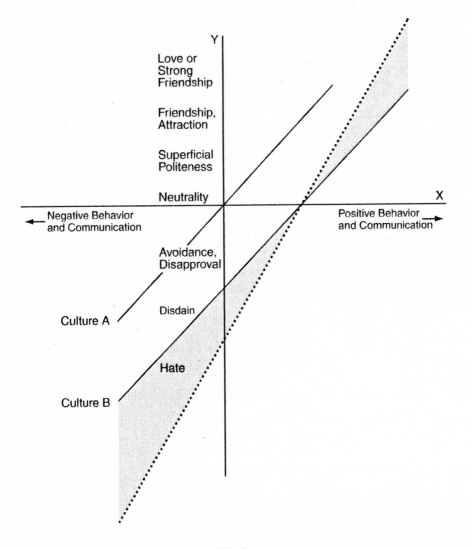

FIG. 1.

The quantity of cooperative behavior or communication between people as well as their negative behavior, can be plotted on the X-axis, while corresponding relationships can be plotted on the Y-axis. With increasingly positive relationships, greater levels of cooperation are performed and vice versa. Hostile relationships will lead to progressively greater levels of antagonistic behavior toward those we dislike in a more or less linear fashion. Absence of behavior has a zero meaning and represents a neutral relationship in the left-shifted Culture A.

In Culture B, a *right shift* has occurred in behavior and its interpretation. On the positive end of the spectrum, this culture requires much greater levels of cooperation and polite communication to maintain positive relationships. On the other end, it assigns very large negative meanings to negative behaviors as well as to a lack of adequate cooperation. Culture B also tends to express both cooperative and antagonistic behaviors indirectly or covertly. These behaviors can be plotted along the Z-axis and called *third-dimensional behaviors* (dotted line). A culture has its own line of interpretation, corresponding line of overt behavior (solid), and associated line of indirect or covert behavior (dotted). In Culture A, behaviors tend to be expressed directly or openly; therefore, little or no Z-axis class behavior exists in this culture—a dotted line is not shown.

While vacationing at the seaside, Frank went from his left-shifted Culture A to a right-shifted society. The gap between his own behavior interpretation system and that of the local residents accounted for many of the observed events during his visit.

Frank was probably grossly mistaken when he perceived the local soccer players' reserved behavior as docile, even incompetent. On the other side, far from being impressed by his stunts, rough play, and pushing, the hosts, based on their right-shifted cultural line, interpreted his actions as very aggressive and barbaric. He was given strong warnings in the form of an absence of communication, frowns, and negative comments, which he misinterpreted as being neutral or only minimally negative.

Absence of communication in his left-shifted cultural environment represented a default mode or standard neutral behavior. He had no perceived reason to anticipate adverse consequences. Conspicuously absent from the behavior of his teammates were praises after his successful actions, which would have been given to a teammate they liked. Due to Frank's left-shifted pattern of interpretation, he failed to understand the negative meaning of this lack of praise.

As predicted by the model, hostile interpretation of Frank's actions led to significant third-dimensional behavior by local people—gossip among the players and others, a refusal to invite the visitor to parties after the game and, ultimately, to the absence of an invitation to participate in another game. His actions and words would likely be remembered for a long time to come, particularly by the goalie. Had further contact occurred between the visitor and locals, this pattern of misinterpretation with its negative consequences would likely have continued to an even greater extent unless, of course, his behavior became significantly right-shifted in the meantime.

The episode with the girl represented another common right-left miscommunication pattern (Fig. 2). Superficial politeness or friendliness she conveyed in her greeting was interpreted by Frank as being more strongly positive behavior—indicating attraction or desire. The visitor's assessment of this behavior as inappropriately suggestive in public would have been correct, had it happened in his own cultural environment. His response was eye contact—a less extensive form of positive communication—which, in turn, led to a common misinterpretation on her part. The response, which was actually positive on a left-shifted line, fell on the neutral portion of her right shifted interpretation. She saw it as a form of rejection! Had further interaction taken place between them, her attitude toward the visitor would have been far less friendly.

The incident on the beach was a similar situation (Fig. 3). The local adolescent, based on his right-shifted cultural line, saw Frank's absence of communication as being arrogant or hateful. In this situation, the individual directly acted upon his observation rather than engage in third-dimensional behavior. Although the reason for this attack was explained to Frank, his persistent belief that it was irrational can be explained by the following analogy: Requiring someone from a left-shifted culture to greet others with a smile or to perform certain other types of positive communication as a daily routine would be like asking a right-shifted resident to perform more extensive forms of positive communication than he is used to performing, such as giving extensive verbal compliments or an embrace. Had someone, for example, expected an embrace and a statement of praise from the local kid and then attacked him if he had failed to comply, he would surely have felt the same way about the event as did Frank, who had been expected to give back a greeting and perhaps, a smile. Some overreaction probably existed in this situation; however, the conflict's underlying basis fits well into a right and left shift model.

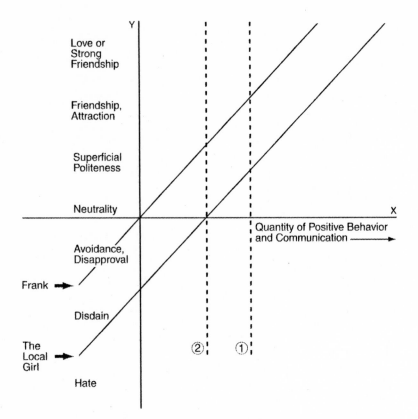

FIG. 2. 1) The girl's gestures meant to convey politeness were interpreted to contain a much greater positive meaning.

2) Frank's positive response was seen as neutrality or rejection.

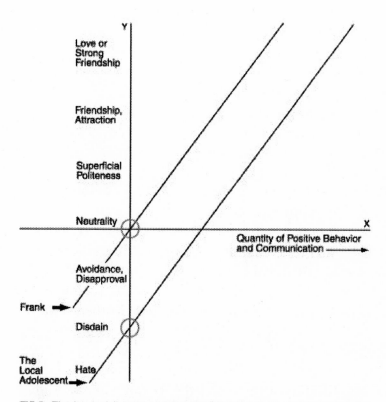

FIG.3. The local adolescent misinterpreted Frank's absence of communication (zero cooperative behavior) as disdain or hate.

DR. T

An INTERNIST MOVED FROM A CULTURALLY LEFT-SHIFTED environment in Texas to a new job at a West Coast teaching hospital. He was a well-respected doctor who had graduated from a prestigious medical school in the top third of his class. His evaluations were generally very good and there were no notable incidents or blemishes to suggest a personality problem or academic deficiency. During a recently completed residency, he received above average evaluations in all categories, including clinical judgment, knowledge, clinical skills, humanistic qualities, and professional attitude. Responsibilities at the new job included clinic work, hospital rounds, conference attendance, and the teaching of residents and medical students. For the first three months, colleagues and other staff members described Dr. T as knowledgeable. They praised his clinical abilities as well as his authoritative lectures. His reviews by residents and medical students were very good.

During the fall of this year, the Texan was spending a night at the hospital on call. He ordered an extensive work up on a recently admitted patient—more than the resident and nursing staff thought was necessary. The nursing supervisor approached Dr. T, asked if frequent blood draws and other tests were really needed, and suggested that the patient be taken off telemetry and transferred to a regular hospital bed. That suggestion was rejected. The supervisor received a lecture about who was the doctor. Dr. T finished his lecture with, "Why don't you go to medical school and get an MD, then you can make these decisions yourself!" This seemed to be the episode's end. The patient did well and was sent home in stable condition after several days.

Later that month, the Texan saw a particularly anxious patient in his clinic who had read a popular magazine article about the use of magnetic resonance imaging (MRI) in diagnosing spinal tumors. The man was worried his back pain could be due to a tumor on his spine and demanded to have an MRI. He had no previous history of cancer, other medical illnesses, or risk factors. The physical examination was normal. Despite receiving assurances that a spinal tumor was very unlikely, with unabated energy, this patient continued to insist on having an MRI. The visit was extended beyond allotted time. In the end, no test was ordered.

Shortly afterwards, Dr. T received a phone call from the patient relations office. He was informed that a complaint had been filed and asked to address the issue. He also had an opportunity to speak with the chief of Quality Assurance, who agreed an MRI was unnecessary, but, given the individual's persistence, ordering it might have been wise to avoid further aggravation to everyone. Eventually this case was handled by someone else because the patient decided to switch physicians.

Other issues were also brought up, including questions about Dr. T's clinical judgment during the on-call admission. Nursing supervisor's version of events was recounted. It appeared that some information about bed and personnel availability had not been given to Dr. T at the time of admission. He successfully defended all decisions he made that night. The need for telemetry was agreed upon. Their conversation ended on a friendly note.

Next several weeks passed with a busy clinic schedule, teaching responsibilities, and hospital rounds. Dr. T gave several authoritative presentations. His statements and suggestions during conferences were generally well received, but during a conference on a Wednesday afternoon, a urologist discussed the follow-up examination of a successfully treated patient. After he presented the history and details of the case, he mentioned how a current CT examination of the abdomen and pelvis was normal, a cystoscopy was normal, and the vagina looked and felt good. Tex then pointed out that it always looks and feels good... There was a loud outburst of laughter. The urologist went silent for a moment, turned pale, then regained his composure and continued with his presentation at somewhat slower pace, knowing he and the joke would be the subject of conversations for some time to come. Dr. T later gave his detailed version of the management history, filling in some gaps left by the urologist.

Most of December passed uneventfully as T remained busy between clinic and hospital duties. Work load was greater during this time. It was fortunate that nurses, transcriptionists, and other staff members were efficient at their jobs. Residents also took very good care of hospitalized patients.

Early in January, a page came from the emergency department for a consultation regarding a possible admission—a case of asthma. The emergency room physician had not done a thorough workup or observed the patient long enough before requesting a consultation. Although recently out of residency and relatively new in the department, he was still relatively weak in a number of areas for someone at that level of training. Physicians from other services frequently spoke amongst each other about his lackluster work. After a brief evaluation, T recognized that with proper treatment and a period of observation in the ER, she could be stabilized and sent home, which would avoid an unnecessary hospital admission. Tex gave the ER physician a lecture on managing asthma and chastised his weak performance. The hospitalization was delayed. It turned out to be a correct decision. After treatment and overnight observation in the emergency department, she was discharged in stable condition.

Soon, Dr. T was invited for a conversation with the chief of staff. Hospital's executive board had met to discuss his case. There had been several reported incidents from the nursing supervisor and other staff members, as well as one from the emergency department. Subjects of reports included overprescription of steroids in cases of emphysema, giving a non-steroidal anti-inflammatory agent to a patient who later developed a gastrointestinal bleed, and delays in consultations. The Texan could hardly believe those accusations. He thought the one about the non-steroidal anti-inflammatory agent was the most ridiculous of all. Occasional gastrointestinal bleeding is a known side effect with such medications and should not preclude their use any more than the occurrence of road accidents should prevent automobile sales. T argued each issue point by point. He was then accused of being uncontrolled and abusive, and warned that further complaints would result in loss of hospital privileges (with loss of employment).

That spring, T made an effort to behave on the conservative side. He avoided controversial situations and management decisions. One tactic was to limit conversations with other physicians, staff members, and patients to only the most polite statements. He became aware of small things, like the careful scrutiny with which the nursing supervisor reviewed chart notes and small glances with cold silence from staff members, which contained more hostility than any quarrel or outburst back in Texas. He saw through the phony smiles and greetings as he learned to go along with it all. The strategies paid off because they left him alone for awhile. It was a great educational experience. Without even noticing, he had made great strides toward becoming one of them.

At the year's end, a new position opened up at a private practice nearby, which he took.

ANALYSIS BASED ON THE THREE-DIMENSIONAL MODEL AGAIN provides a more thorough understanding of the events. Physicians, as a group, are a relatively right-shifted population; however, within this group, significant variation exists based on geography, socioeconomic background, genetic predisposition and other factors that reflects variations in the general population. Upon moving to his new location on the West Coast, Dr. T found himself in a significantly more right-shifted culture than the population he was used to.

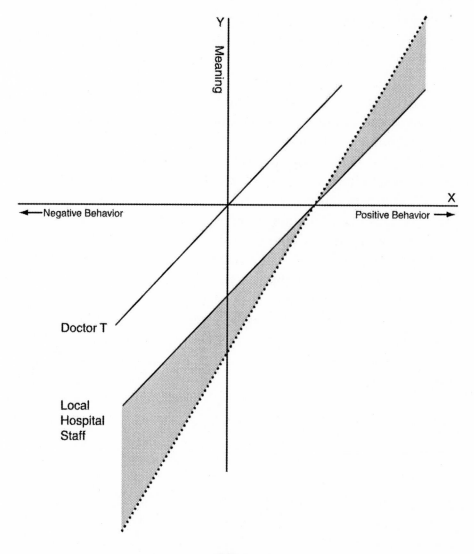

FIG. 4.

Coming from an environment in which a mild negative relationship is expressed with direct verbal confrontation, he applied this form of communication in his interaction with the nursing supervisor. The perceived magnitude of negative meaning was far greater than intended because the nursing supervisor understood it based on a right-shifted line of interpretation. To the Texan, this incident represented the end of a successful argument. To the supervisor, it meant the start of war. As predicted by the model, subsequent response was large in magnitude and duration, and consisted mostly of indirect, covert actions which, in a hospital setting, generally revolve around accusations of harassment, clinical incompetence, mismanagement, incomplete work-ups, misdiagnoses, etc. In another place and time, the doctor might have found himself reported to secret police and accused of political conspiracy, fraud, or practicing witchcraft. As it turned out, this vengeful third-dimensional behavior lasted several months.

Teasing comments (the kind described during Wednesday's conference) have a very large negative meaning in right-shifted societies. A light joke and other remarks soon forgotten by the Texan would be remembered by the urologist as a major insult to his character that would require a serious retribution.

The situation in the emergency department was a similar case. Most of ER physician's colleagues had low opinions of him, but expressed them in an indirect manner and avoided placing themselves in harm's way. Paradoxically, the Texan, whose thoughts and intentions toward the ER physician were among the most benign, provoked a very hostile reaction simply because he lacked awareness about the meaning of a direct verbal confrontation in this environment.

The episode with the clinic patient who requested an MRI is a common experience encountered by most physicians in practice. Patients with persistent irrational demands represent only a small segment of the general public, but they exist in adequate numbers to pose a frequent challenge to even the most experienced practitioners. Perhaps a physician more acclimated to the local population would have spent more time with this patient to accomplish more positive communication and avoid a direct confrontation. With awareness of the potential for hostility in this environment, such a physician might have given in and ultimately ordered an MRI to avoid subsequent actions taken by the patient.

Dr. T, being from a left-shifted culture, did not comprehend the significance of this failure to reach an agreement and cooperate with the patient's demands.

Absence of agreement in a right-shifted context is equivalent to absence of communication or cooperation (zero positive behavior). It has a strongly negative meaning with major consequences, including extensive indirect and covert retaliations. Right-shifted societies generally develop institutions and offices to deal with third-dimensional behavior (attenuate its effects). In this case, it is the patient relations office.

Problems arise when cultural right shift progresses to an extent at which the magnitude of negative relationships and Z-axis class behaviors generated from everyday encounters outstrips these institutions' abilities to handle them. Such a situation can lead to extensive covert hostilities outside the system, which can end with unpredictable consequences.

Accusations of uncontrolled behavior from the chief of staff were understandable because there is a common tendency in right-shifted cultures to mistakenly view lower aspects of left-shifted behavior as being caused by excessive hostility and absence of moderation. In a rightward-oriented place, where the lowest acceptable negative conduct may be silence, actions such as verbal confrontation and arguing are off the scale. In such a cultural context, the amount of negative emotion necessary to express this behavior openly is so great, it can well require an absence of control or an irrational mind. By contrast, in a left-shifted environment, arguing is generally an orderly and acceptable form of communication at lower ends of the spectrum. It is equivalent to what silence would mean in the aforementioned right-shifted place... In order to find a left-shifted behavior that would correspond to a quarrel or verbal confrontation in a right-oriented society, one would have to go further down the left line of interpretation (Figure 4) and find more extensive verbal threats, physical violence, etc. Had the Texan behaved in this manner, it might have indicated an irrational frame of mind or loss of control.

People targeted by third-dimensional behavior will often argue point-by-point against various indirect accusations, without realizing that the real origin of hostility aimed at them may be hidden in a small conflict or even inadequate cooperation sometime before.

Dr. T's perception of smiles and positive gestures as being phony is a common one. Left-shifted individuals and groups interpret such behavior as indicative of strong friendship and/or attraction. When they find it does not mean what they think it does, it is seen as false, deceitful, or pretentious. As a rule, however, this behavior is genuine, but it has a *different meaning* in right-shifted cultures. It represents the quantity of co-operative behavior necessary to maintain neutral relationships. Its meaning is very real—its presence is required to keep proper relations and prevent hostility.

As frequently happens, the man adjusted to his situation out of necessity. He introduced a rigid step to block out the lower part of his behavior spectrum and increased his positive communication. He actually imposed a partial right shift on himself. Such a strategy can be effective provided that adequate good will remains from other staff members. It did prove to be useful in Dr. T's case.

Further adjustment to this new environment might include the introduction of additional knowledge that would complete his interpretation along a more right-sided line and displacing behaviors away from the X-Y plane into the third dimension. The process would gradually leave a narrow range of positive behavior displayed in public—that which is necessary to maintain neutral relationships.

Like other outsiders who go through a culture shock because their behavior interpretation lines are disrupted, the Texan would probably go through many more misinterpretations, underactions, overactions, etc., prior to narrowing his frame of mind into a more linear pattern that matches his new society's demands.

GEORGE AND THE REVOLUTION

GEORGE WAS THE THIRD SON BORN IN AN EXTENDED FAMILY IN A northern rural society where generations of the same household lived and worked together. Parents and older children labored in the fields while grandparents cared for the younger kids. Their house had three large rooms and it was flanked by two smaller one-room houses in which older sons lived with their wives. The arrangement was average for peasants of this country and time. During this relatively quiet, prosperous period, landowners helped them build a new home.

Overlooking the area was a housing complex where landowners lived in a similar, but smaller, family arrangement. Their eldest son was gradually taking over responsibilities from his father, which included land management, supervision of peasants, and defending their common interests.

George's family was among the owners' favorites. They did their work well, often beyond what was expected, and without having to be told what to do all the time. In exchange, they received many privileges. Beyond the help with house building, two daughters were allowed to work as maids at the owners' estate and their children were often invited to the playground. At a young age, George received money to help pay for his move to the southern peninsula where he took a factory job. Few Northerners, at this time, paid attention to a revolutionary movement in the south, which had gained momentum.

Being fresh and able-bodied when he entered the work force, George was immediately put onto twelve-hour shifts. Although the labor was exhausting, he enjoyed his new niche because it provided financial independence, as well as a large support group of friends and coworkers who introduced him to the revolutionary movement and recruited him into several related organizations. Over a period of three years, George participated in meetings, distributed pamphlets, and worked to convert new followers. He was caught up in the excitement of the movement, which had as its principal goal the liberation and advancement of underprivileged classes. Rude bureaucrats would no longer be allowed to sit around wasting time while people stood in dingy hallways waiting to see them. A particularly appealing idea was the notion of an egalitarian society that could provide a fair distribution of wealth; without beating, yelling, reprimands, or bosses who looked over the workers' shoulders all day.

George was greatly motivated because of his own situation and also because he wanted to help his folks in the north. If successful, revolutionary party had promised to help peasants gain freedom from the landowners. George gradually came to see the latter class for what they were—violent users and oppressors of his family. His resolve grew steadily. He planned to become one of thousands of men who would volunteer to join the revolutionary army.

Organizational meetings and planning sessions were held mostly in secret. Help came from many powerful intellectuals who were fed up with the entrenched regime's barbaric methods. They often came to participate in disguise, under assumed names to avoid detection and harassment from authorities.

George knew that the beginning of rebellion with a formal takeover of ruling institutions was set for August 18. This knowledge was supposed to be limited to the revolutionary leadership, but information trickled out by word of mouth—it soon became a widely known secret. It would be a hot summer for everyone, particularly the upper classes whose oppression was responsible for the majority's frustration.

That spring, George traveled with his fiancée back to the home town for a short visit. Almost four years had passed since he had last seen his relatives. Family house and older brothers' homes seemed miniature now. Even the owner's estate looked small compared to what he remembered. Younger sisters had matured greatly—one was married with a two-year old son named George—after him. The kid even looked like his uncle. Older brothers' children had also grown. They were almost as tall as their parents and just as excited to see George. The welcome given to him and the future bride was a truly memorable one. She immediately became a part of the family. For two weeks, they were allowed to feel carefree as they laughed, sang, and danced into the night. George would remember this visit as the happiest time of his life. Prior to couple's return trip, relatives gathered hand-crafted textiles and home decorations as wedding presents, little knowing it would be a long time before the recipients would have a chance to use them.

The war broke out only days later. August eighteenth rumor, as it turned out, was a disinformation planted by revolutionary leadership. It caught the bourgeoisie off guard. Along with most of his friends from work, George joined the revolutionary army and quickly saw action against loyalist forces. His skill and leadership qualities allowed him to steadily rise through the ranks.

Revolutionary army's military success would match its party's political success as bastions of the old regime rapidly fell before determined men. Within several months, revolutionary leadership established control over most southern regions. They were now poised to march northward, where die-hard remnants of urban ruling class had allied with landowners in an attempt to reverse these gains. Since public relations efforts were largely unsuccessful among rural population, peasants who didn't, or wouldn't, understand that the revolutionary army was on their side, fought alongside ruling classes. Such a composition of northern forces presented a formidable challenge. Despite outdated tactics and relatively poor coordination, they managed to hold out for two years before revolutionary forces gained the decisive victories. Superior coordination and organization, as well as greater weapons production, ultimately decided the outcome.

George became a captain near the war's end. His unit moved to occupy an area that included his own village for a rare opportunity to be reunited with family while in wartime service. He found them alive and well. His oldest brother had been recruited into the northern army which fortunately surrendered before he saw action. Everyone was happy to see them both, regardless of their uniform.

Revolutionary party and senior officers found George to be a useful liaison in establishing rapport with local population. Foremost on their agenda was redistribution of land and owners' property to the peasants.

Landowners, among whom was George's former landlord, and others from the old regime were put on public trial. Driven by inertia, George decided to see this event. By now, his anger had faded. Before him stood a broken man in his late forties on whom the war had taken a great toll.

Several peasants, encouraged by the revolutionary tribunal, came forward to testify about abuses suffered at the hands of the accused. They indicated in clear terms how they felt about the beatings, long hours of forced labor, and denial of wages. A picture began to emerge of a harsh, malevolent individual who frequently abused his power, exploited the peasants, and caused quite a bit of hardship among the population he controlled. During most of the trial he stood silent, barely uttering a word in his own defense. His wife tried to defend them both, recalling their help to the poor, homes built for other families, the celebrations, and all the good times they had together. To her it was inconceivable these people would turn against them. Yes, they had beaten the peasants, but it wasn't like *that*—it was more the way a parent would beat a child. No harm was ever intended.

She told the crowd, "My husband was the best friend you had. He loved you!" She accused the tribunal members of teaching hate. "All you have brought us is discontent...I haven't seen a single peasant sing or dance since your trials began. These people used to be happy before you came here!"

A judge scoffed at her speech and pointed out that she was talking about a degradation of adults, not children. He regarded it as another blatant attempt to justify a corrupt system. Who could expect people to be abused while working in the fields under miserable conditions and sing and dance about it?

Toward the trial's end, two maids came forward with accusations of rape. Since most claims were determined to be valid, the landowner was sentenced to death by hanging. His property was later distributed among local peasants and his wife moved away—a quick, surprisingly easy end to a once powerful household.

After the trials and land redistribution, George received a transfer to the South, where he was reunited with his wife. In the subsequent years, they had two sons. Both boys breezed through school with excellent academic records. George remained in the service to achieve the rank of colonel before retirement. His sons attended college and later became successful in their own careers. At a relatively young age, his wife died of heart disease, which ran in her family. After her passing, he steadily turned to old comrades-in-arms for companionship and often sat in the park to reminisce about the revolution.

Northern relatives occasionally visited for several days at a time. During one stopover, his brother mentioned that a neighbor's daughter, who was coming down south to study at the university, needed a place to stay. George was happy to help since her parents were longtime friends. She would be welcomed in the house as one of his own.

Tamara moved in at the end of the summer. She was somewhat more emancipated than country girls the colonel remembered—a kid from the internet generation, open and outgoing, with mannerisms that displayed confidence. She stayed out late and listened to loud music. Her many friends called on the phone all day long. She talked to and went out with several boys. "Such behavior used to be reserved for the one person you loved, not half the city," George thought. "Back in the old days, her parents would have given her a good beating." Nevertheless, he tried hard to maintain good relations and refrained from scolding the child too often.

Most bothersome were frequent late-night phone calls that kept him awake, even though she spoke on a separate line in her room. One evening, while she was out, her telephone rang for some time. George gathered his audacity and walked into the room to pick up the phone.

"Hello."

"Hello, I need to speak with Tamara, please."

"Who are you?"

"This is Tamara's boyfriend."

"Well, which one?" chuckled George.

There was a brief silence on the other end. "All right," he continued, "give me your number and I'll have her call you."

The next night, George was up late again, thanks to persistent calls. This time he stayed around waiting and, as soon as Tamara walked in after midnight, started with a lecture about her habits and manners. His speech evoked little response. In fact, she casually opened a closet door and began to hang up her clothes, seemingly oblivious to his words.

George walked up from behind and took her by the shoulder, "Listen, turn around and look at me when I'm talking to you." Her response was greater than he expected. She jumped back and swiftly walked to her room, locking the door behind her. As communication stopped there, George didn't press the issue any further.

Tamara departed early the following day. The retired colonel went out later to have lunch with friends—engaged in

25

same conversations, but punctuated by a recounting of the previous night's episode. George recalled the vigorous arguments he always had with his wife. Spouses threatened and fought, but still cared for each other immensely. A certain freedom existed in their ability to act out and still maintain a relationship. He couldn't understand these hypersensitive people who allowed one little disagreement to lead to endless retributions. A friend mentioned how younger generations would need another revolution to put things into perspective. The group laughed about it.

Later that afternoon, Tamara was busy with her brother and a young friend moving her belongings out of the house. They hardly spoke. From the way they looked at George, one would have thought he had assaulted her. She left without saying goodbye.

After months of liveliness, the old man's home became quiet again. In a way, he would miss the music and the phone calls. He played his radio loudly to drown out the silence at night. Regular meetings with comrades-in-arms went on... All agreed their fellow veteran was right and extended him full moral support, as they had before.

Two days later, it happened—policemen showed up at George's door. Interrogations about the incident began. He was taken out in full view of his neighbors and driven to the station where officers turned up the pressure to make him confess. "To what?" he wondered, "Having tolerated the brat for a semester?" Cops insisted their main objective was to make sure such an incident wouldn't happen to anyone else—the verbal threats which culminated in physical assault.

George was beside himself. The old system hadn't arrested him for plotting a coup; now, this was happening... A few years earlier, he would have shown them what a physical assault was!

Interrogations were as exhausting as any battle. The captive was finally released on his own recognizance, but he knew that the damage was already done in an intangible way because his neighborhood had changed over time. In times past, an arrest over a fighting incident would be hardly noticed. Nowadays, a person couldn't do so much as frown without someone being appalled. In short, people had been free to act out while police had the freedom to arrest them. These liberties were fast disappearing. *The observers* had taken over—a class that paid attention to every detail, every inconsistency, and the slightest sign of disagreement. George knew well this incident would become a permanent subject. Neighbors would welcome his arrest like a pack of hungry wolves welcomed a lamb chop—his past service and rank mattered little to busybodies.

It hurt to know that accusations came from Tamara's whole family who had turned sour after being friends for so long and everything he had done for them. The whole ordeal bore an eerie resemblance to events during the revolutionary trials; it was almost the landowner's downfall revisited. But this experience was different. Now, the accused hadn't done anything to the peasants…in his own mind, at least.

George was an old soldier intent on fighting oppression, though. They would still hear about it—the police, his neighbors, and the ingrates who were out to ruin his reputation. To the end, he would continue to make a small individual contribution to society's right shift.

THE THREE-DIMENSIONAL MODEL AGAIN PROVIDES MEANINGFUL insight into major forces that influenced events during the protagonist's life. George moved from a left-shifted northern environment to a more competitive right-shifted one in the south. His gradual reinterpretation of landowners' behavior as being sadistic and outrageous was based on his new culture's line, which assigned a very large negative meaning to small signs of negative behavior. Y-axis location of these behaviors became shifted downward in George's mind. The yelling and beating, which he once understood as acceptable actions with a moderate negative meaning, now became seen as major human rights violations.

Revolutionary party's crusade against physical and verbal abuse represents a major increment in the negative block component of behavioral right shift. *Negative block* refers to a prohibition of overt expression of negative relationship-defining behaviors. This process occurs in small daily increments, larger steps, and periodic giant public policy strokes, such as a zero-tolerance policy. As a short-term measure, they can work well; however, over prolonged time periods in competitive situations, these steps increase the natural selection pressure to favor individuals and groups who are able to develop indirect or covert types of aggression. A gradual redistribution of interpretation occurs along more right-shifted lines. Then, third-dimensional behavior develops, which can actually lead to more hostility at the end of the whole process than what was originally in place. The situation becomes even more tenuous because the threshold for establishing negative relationships is now lower due to a redistributed interpretation pattern. In addition, aggression is expressed indirectly or covertly, which makes it more difficult to identify and suppress in time, if at all.

Redistribution of interpretation makes zero-tolerance an open-ended proposition.

Difficulties with zero-tolerance and other negative block policies arise from an inability to establish a finite set of behaviors targeted for exclusion. The set of negative-relationship-defining behaviors that trigger exclusionary policies constantly shifts to the right to involve progressively lower quantities of negative behavior and, ultimately, inadequate quantities of positive behavior.

First, the physically violent barbarians are eliminated. Then, the redistribution moves to exclude those who argue and threaten. Next on the list are people who remain silent, refusing to cooperate. They are now perceived as barbarians entrenched below society's tolerance level. Once they are finished, new interpretation progresses to target those who are not cooperative *enough,* and so forth. This process is repeated over and over until it results in a society filled with hypersensitive people who react furiously to the slightest lack of cooperation and, with advancing third-dimension behavior, use extensive indirect, covert strategies to express their aggression.

Legal systems and other institutions make a conscious effort to maintain stable responses to negative-relationship-defining behaviors. Nature, however, does not. In the long run, dynamics of common interaction favor those who are perceived to be on the positive side of Y-axis. Reacting naturally to events around us, we arrest criminals, punish those who threaten us, complain about rude clerks, demand politeness, and reward the good people who help us, unwittingly making a small contribution to society's right shift all the time.

Conspiracy represents cooperative third-dimensional behavior—along positive aspects of the Z-axis. It is abundant in right-oriented environments. As predicted by the 3-D model, a right-shifted interpretation and behavior pattern in the south led to extensive covert and indirect cooperation that gave rise to covert organizations. In this case, it was the revolutionary party with its related organizations, secret societies, etc. Disgruntled intellectuals who challenged the ruling classes did so indirectly through workers and revolutionary organizations rather than personally and openly, which is consistent with the prediction of extensive amount of third-dimensional behavior coming from right-shifted cultural groups. Negative indirect and covert behaviors from these groups (planning the armed revolt, acquisition of weapons, propaganda, etc.) had outstripped the existing institutions' abilities to handle their consequences.

After a successful revolution, a war occurred between the relatively right-shifted southern society and a left-shifted north. When other factors are more or less equal (resources, manpower, etc.), the population with a more right-shifted average line of interpretation has the upper hand in a conflict. Such a population requires more cooperative behavior to establish positive and neutral relationships. This society's army would be expected to require a higher performance level from its soldiers, as well as to engage in more elaborate maneuvers, which would give it a battlefield advantage. Its high demands for cooperation would predictably yield greater weapons productions and superior output of other manufactured goods. Eventually, these factors would come together to hand a victory to the right-shifted culture.

During the revolutionary trials, landowners faced a situation where the lower end of their leftward behavior was being judged against the tribunal's right-shifted interpretation. Local peasants, who once accepted verbal reprimands and even beatings as normal events, and took them relatively lightly, were learning, under the revolutionary party's influence, to assign strong negative meanings to negative behaviors. The argument, "We beat them, but it wasn't meant to hurt them," shows a difference in the cultural perception of this particular behavior. The three-dimensional model indicates that variations in interpretation of this behavior represent only a small part of a much greater picture that involves a linear shift from the most positive to the most negative ends.

With regard to Tamara, a very sensitive character George encountered, it should be understood that positive meaning of cooperative behavior and communication progressively decreases with a cultural right shift. It eventually approaches neutrality and even falls below neutrality. This expectation includes interaction between opposite sexes; therefore, behaviors which designate strong affection in a left-shifted rural society (positive communication, dating, cooperation on tasks, etc.), become standard, everyday conduct with little or no positive meaning. What used to be reserved for the one person someone loved is extended to a large number of people. Its positive value approaches zero level on the Y-axis.

On the behavior spectrum's other end, Tamara's generation assigns large negative meanings to relatively small quantities of negative behavior. Whereas it once took extensive threats, beatings and yelling (strongly explicit signs of aggression) to establish a very negative relationship, nowadays, only a few negative comments and slight physical contact can produce the same level of hostility. In the future, with a further cultural right shift, it may only take a brief sideways glance indicating negative thought process to set up this type of antagonistic meaning with all its associated consequences. As predicted by the model, Tamara's reaction was greater than George expected and it was accompanied by extensive third-dimensional behaviors—mainly indirect actions against him through her friends, family and the police. Ironically, George had realized he was dealing with a sensitive person. He tried to adjust by blocking out many negative behaviors, but he still grossly underestimated the situation—the right shift had surpassed his efforts to compensate.

By contrast, George's relationship with his wife was left-shifted, so large quantities of negative communication were taken lightly. Neither spouse became very upset or hateful toward the other after an argument. The default mode in their relationship was more or less an absence of communication, while relatively low levels of cooperation and positive language were enough to establish positive sentiments. Such relationships are easier to maintain than the right-shifted ones, which demand constant positive communication and cooperation to preserve even neutral attitudes. This phenomenon can be largely credited for keeping George and his wife together for a lifetime despite the superficial appearance of a dysfunctional marriage.

One last look at George's arrest... The society's advancing rightward interpretation trends caused this event to acquire a very serious negative meaning, which carries rumors, social disgrace, and third-dimensional behaviors. The freedom to be arrested without significant consequences to one's reputation and well-being is disappearing in George's neighborhood and around the world. Had George been younger—trying to establish a career—these consequences would have been even more detrimental in terms of potential job loss and other forms of ostracism. Ultimately, they could add up to cause far more harm to one's well-being than a brief arrest or a punch in the face in a left-minded cultural context.

Interestingly, since cultural right shift is an across-the-board phenomenon, it would progressively affect the police as well as George. They might face charges from him or other concerned citizens about brutality, abuse, procedural mistakes, misconduct, and many other allegations. Such actions would probably come indirectly through the legal system, the media, an internal investigations office, or other organizations and require less and less actual provocation from the involved officers to precipitate. Some citizens might also act covertly outside the system.

Without realizing it, by reacting to negative events, George would continue to fuel the very process that worked to ruin his reputation—the right shift.

This phenomenon can be broken down into four principal components:

1. Negative block;
2. Increase in cooperation and positive communication;
3. Redistribution of interpretation; and
4. Acquisition of indirect and covert behavior patterns.

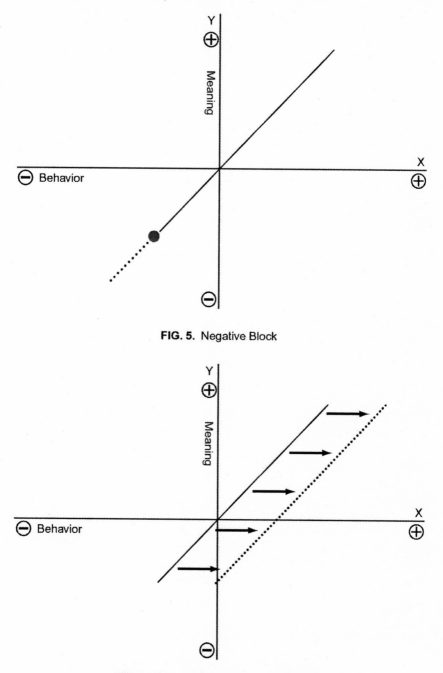

FIG. 5. Negative Block

FIG. 6. Demand for Greater Cooperation

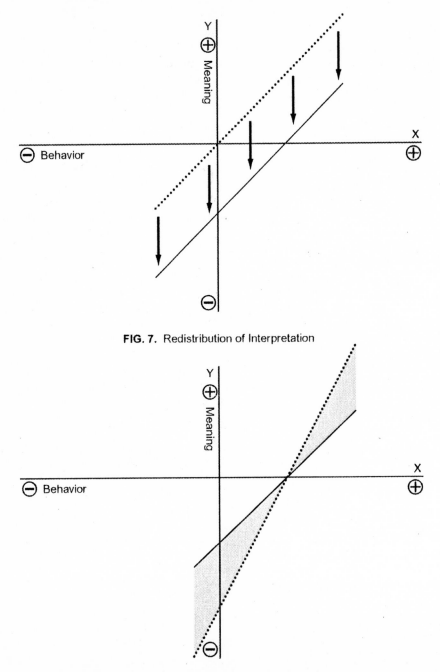

FIG. 7. Redistribution of Interpretation

FIG. 8. Advent of Third-Dimensional Behavior Patterns

MARTIAN AURORA

FROM THE TIME THEIR ANCESTORS *TERRAFORMED* MARS, MARTIAN population thrived in a cultural middle ground, maintaining a healthy balance between savage ways of the Deimen people, whose ancestors were the earliest colonists from Earth, and restrictive excesses of modern *terran* newcomers.

The Martians, faced with population pressures from Earth, allowed a continuous, low-level space immigration. This controlled invasion benefited both sides. Martian policymakers figured the earthmen would come anyway, by force if they wanted. Through immigration they would be given a fair opportunity to become patriotic citizens and contribute to the economy. In any case, newcomers already held key posts in bureaucratic institutions, which gave them substantial power to fend for themselves.

Native Martians who wanted to see reduced immigration levels placed their hopes in the increasingly sophisticated population planning techniques on Earth. Cycles of population peaks alternated with periods of reproductive restriction like giant waves gradually slowing over centuries to approach a coveted zero-growth baseline.

Martian emigration acted as a safety valve of sorts for those wealthy enough to afford it or fortunate enough to win the space travel lottery. Martian cynics complained that political agitators and crooks of every kind won the lottery far too frequently. Whoever they were, though, Mars for them was a planet of opportunity—a place where one could make it big, build a new life, or both.

The second continuous migration period was a time span between two great space travel disruptions which defined true

Martian ancestry. The first cessation, caused by an act of nature, lasted one hundred-fifty earth years and separated Martians from Deimen. The latter population owed its name to a small nine-by-seven-mile asteroid moon Deimos where their ancestors left a refueling base first encountered by new travelers on their way to recolonize Mars. The second wave of colonists brought about the planet's greatest progress. They painstakingly melted its polar caps with solar and nuclear power, increased its atmospheric density, and introduced an ionosphere to protect the surface from harmful ultraviolet radiation, making the environment completely habitable. Their technology transformed a planet of bubble dwellers and greenhouse farmers into a really modern civilization. The next great disruption lasted almost one hundred earth years and was an act of man. It lasted long enough to culturally separate Martians from the latest newcomers.

Salien's ancestors were considered to be true Martians because they arrived during the second continuous migration period. They were a long line of hard-working, upper-middle class professionals. His father was a satellite engineer who invested in stocks and made a comfortable living. He instilled in his son a strong work ethic and spent long hours with him studying algebra and physics. This experience gave the kid a good head start in preparation for college.

Following in his father's footsteps, Salien obtained a degree in mechanical engineering at the Martian age of eleven. He graduated from Tharsis University and took a job in automobile design. Engineering was one of the most prestigious careers even though its financial rewards were mediocre. In addition to his work, Salien took an active interest in stocks and gradually became engrossed in the same papers his father had mulled over all his life.

One of perennially stable institutions that survived centuries of political change and natural disasters was the stock market—people loved to invest regardless of planetary circumstances. It held the promise of financial rewards that could greatly exceed what one could make working on a salary. It also provided opportunities for early retirement. While the society meticulously fostered beliefs in long-term investment as an optimal route toward collective prosperity and most media discouraged fast trading as well as other get-rich-quick schemes, which were considered a dishonorable way to make a living, increasing numbers of solid citizens turned away from their careers to try their luck and wisdom in the market.

Salien worked in automobile design for two years and progressively embarked on stocks to augment his income. Since trading activities interfered with his job, he had put in for an extended leave. Working from home for a while promised to be a financially and spiritually rewarding experience.

At his office, he turned on the market news channel for an early update. A young anchorman appeared on the screen with charts and monitors lined across the room behind him.

"Join us this afternoon at fourteen-thirty for a live interview with the CEO of Solar Satellite Network."

Salien smiled. It was the company for which his late father had worked. He figured the news had to be good; otherwise, there would be little reason for the CEO to show up. The only question was how much would this stock rise after the news. It was a popular entity with a recently slumping value. He figured there was no place for it to go but up. He checked the SSN chart on his computer, placed an electronic order to buy ten thousand shares and turned to continue with paperwork.

At 11:15, Salien's pager went off. It was from Jules, a friend from college. They arranged to meet for lunch at the club around noon. Salien finished up with work as he periodically checked on stock reports. He left his office at 11:45 and went to the club to find Jules waiting for him in the front lobby. They gave each other a warm greeting. Jules was also an engineer who worked across town. Both of them had an interest in the market, but for Salien, it had become more than a hobby. He kept that information to himself for now.

"How are you doing?" Jules asked. "I called your office twice. You weren't there."

"When, today?"

"In the last couple of days, actually," he said

"I've been in and out. The place slows me down quite a bit." Salien began to set the stage to eventually announce an exit.

"Maybe you should think about a sabbatical or a new position." Jules had beaten him to it.

"Good to hear that from you…and a little surprising."

They walked past the heavy oak tables to their favorite spot and took a seat. A large, hand-woven red carpet was the latest item hung on the wall across from them. Jules took a long look at it.

"There is more *kitsch* in here every day…" He was right.

What was once a private club for a carefully screened society of prominent Martians now accepted everyone who agreed to pay a membership fee and everything they brought in with them. The club was full of Martians who acted like Deimen, bearded men playing chess and poker, artists, and even Deimen. About the only people who didn't venture in were upper-class Earthmen. They kept busy with their own culture clubs and lived in communities distinguished by a constant demand for perfection, protected by an endless array of surveillance devices.

Jules felt an admiration for the Earth's elite with a touch of envy. He emulated them in every way and tried to live up to their standards, believing they represented a role model for Martian future. Derision of the *kitsch*, the Deimen, and other less-than-noble elements at the club was largely a part of living up to the image of earthmen in his own mind. Virtually all of it was just talk. His bark was really much worse than his bite. Salien understood this well and liked him for it. Although their political views were quite opposite on many issues, Salien firmly believed that his friend was a liberal deep inside, far

38

closer to Deimen and the bearded card players than he ever wanted to admit. The mere fact that he often spoke his mind out loud, even if to say something ridiculously negative, made him a model of expressive freedom in which Salien believed.

The waiter, a Deimen with sunken eyes and rows of wrinkles across his forehead, welcomed the two with a stoic look. A Band-Aid ran across his cheek where he had cut himself shaving. Salien was comfortable with it. He tolerated the Deimen as long as they tolerated him. The men ordered their meals and went on with the conversation as they periodically checked their watches. After a while, Jules became somewhat impatient and made eye contact with the waiter, pointing to his watch. Twenty minutes passed before their orders arrived. By this time, both men were anxious to get back to work. They hastily finished their meals and asked for their check.

On his way out, Jules turned to the waiter: "That's okay. You don't need to say, 'Hello,' or 'Goodbye,' or thank me for the tip." The man gave him a blank stare, barely aware of his comments.

Salien nudged his friend toward the door. "Leave it alone. That's just the way they are," he said.

"Someone ought to teach them how to behave."

"Just leave it. He doesn't owe you a greeting."

Besides having a soft spot for Deimen, Salien made it a personal policy to avoid offending people who served him food.

"They'll set a bad example for the rest of us; poor manners, always looking for the easy way out. We're starting to look and act just like them," Jules argued.

"It doesn't bother me. Besides, look how tolerant these people are. You couldn't talk like that to someone from Earth."

Jules gave the waiter one last look and walked out. The men arranged for their next get-together, then parted to go back to work.

That afternoon, Salien kept a watch on the SSN stock. It rose four percent after the good news reported during the public appearance of company's CEO. It finished strong at the end of the session and he decided to hold on to it overnight, expecting its rise to continue early the next day from an influx of buy orders.

Another stock he had observed for several days was the RRL. Its initial period showed a steep rise of 600 percent, which was later followed by a fast slide back to baseline. Temptation to buy in on the upswing was there. The difficult part was knowing when to get out. With his luck, he could easily buy at the very peak and ride its decline into the ground. He looked at RRL's history for a while. The chart resembled a spectrophotometry graph with its slightly jagged, but steady baseline punctuated by spikes of 500 percent or higher— somewhat unusual... RRL was a trendy restaurant chain that periodically hosted celebrity performances. If one could only predict when its peaks would occur and invest beforehand. It dawned on him that celebrity events might account for those peaks. The publicity would attract promises of investment, which may prompt its value to rise over a baseline maintained by a loyal group of investors.

Salien checked the dates of recent peaks against news about RRL. Two of the peaks did coincide with performances by celebrity entertainers; one did not. He conceived a straightforward plan to capitalize on this stock. He would buy twenty thousand shares at baseline, worth almost four months of an engineer's salary, wait for the price to start soaring and sell during the buying frenzy—hopefully near its peak. But this plan had to wait for the SSN stock to be sold first.

Salien decided to take the last two days off work. He drove home to find his kids busy in their rooms—daughter was with her friends and son was typing a homework assignment on the computer, or so it seemed. His wife came home from work later on. They had dinner just prior to bedtime, which made sleeping difficult. One benefit of a controlled planetary atmosphere was life in a convertible home without an unpleasant surprise by a storm. Salien opened the roof on their side of the house and lay for a long time under an open sky, thinking about the day ahead.

He woke up early with anticipation of continued profits. He felt a certain guilt as he turned on the computer. This very much qualified as fast trading the society discouraged. His ancestors were career professionals who would have never quit a job to embark on something so close to gambling. What made someone do it? Maybe it was the profits, maybe the lifestyle— an ability to make more money before noon than he would in a week employed as an engineer. Perhaps the free time was a large incentive, but there was something else, too. Society had become less hostile toward negative conduct. Behaviors that were once considered to be a major disgrace were now merely something to laugh at. Salien liked the idea because to him it meant more freedom. Still, he kept it in the family for the present time. His friends, particularly Jules, would likely give him hell if they knew.

The market opened on a sour note. SSN was down 4 percent, which wiped out all of previous day's gains. Salien felt cheated. A rational decision at the moment would have been to sell and cut the losses, but he held on, hoping for a turnaround. The freefall continued, however. Each update brought the stock's value down. Within an hour, it was down 15 percent! With a sinking feeling, he sold all shares and sat back looking at the screen for a few moments. There was an irresistible urge to recover the money. Further updates of SSN indicated a slight rise in its value from 44.20 to 44.40, then to 44.60. This was it! The recovery had started. He bought the stock at 45.10 and anxiously awaited an upturn. Dreadfully, however, the trend reversed. Once again, he was caught in a slide, hoping for a recovery. The price went down to 43.20 in five minutes. He wanted to sell again but decided to hold on for a while longer. The decline continued to 41.00, then to 39. He finally sold it again at 38.30.

It took some time for the effect to fully sink in—a loss of two months' salary before noon. What a time to have quit work! Salien walked downstairs, numb from defeat, took out a beer, and watched the TV for a while. When he went back upstairs and checked on SSN again, it was up to 43.50. The whole market was on its way up. He thought about another try at a purchase, but felt certain that prices would plummet the moment he did.

There was a lot of free time at hand and, even under the circumstances, Salien went for a game of tennis and a jog in the afternoon. The exercise helped. Still, feelings of loss lingered through the weekend.

The next week brought renewed hopes of recovery. He stayed on a conservative road and quick-traded low-volatility stocks for small profit. At this rate, it would be possible to make up for the losses within a few weeks. High risk transactions were off the menu for now, except for... He kept thinking about RRL. No celebrity events were planned for the near future. Still, he had inklings about this stock and placed an order to buy twenty thousand shares as he continued to trade low-volatility power company stocks.

RRL's baseline remained steady for about two days. Other investments were stable. By that week's end, Salien regained a significant portion of his loss and managed to teach his son to follow market news in case he needed help.

Late on Friday, he took his wife out to the club for a regular visit. Several friends were already there. They sat outside for a while and enjoyed the sunset from a warm patio. Suddenly, the club's relative tranquility was interrupted by what sounded like ducks quarreling. They turned around to see three Deimen engaged in a melee—yelling, shoving, and hitting each other. The three quickly took their ruckus outside. Most guests looked at each other for a moment, then burst into laughter. A supervisor appeared on the scene to take down details of the event and interview witnesses—a pedantic young bureaucrat, tanned, without a glitch on his face or clothes; probably second or third generation from Earth. Salien focused on the man's haircut to look for any hairs out of place. There were none.

Someone spoke out, "They're just Deimen, for God's sake, let them sort it out!" The *terran*, however, continued with his inquiry.

A car passed near the entrance a little while later with the three combatants inside—apparently back at their baseline.

Early Monday began uneventfully as Salien continued to quick-trade low-risk stocks for conservative profits. His son had become quite good at looking up quotes. Tuesday's activities went smoothly. Later that afternoon, the kid walked into his father's room.

"I hear someone at the door," he announced.

"I'll get it. Go on and do your work."

Jules was in front with his wife and brother-in-law. They happened to be in the neighborhood. People had largely dispensed with their ancestral custom of calling before a planned visit.

"I'm surprised to find you here. I thought you were still at work," Jules said. "Is Diana here?"

"She'll be home any minute. Come on in."

Salien took them into his living room and opened the roof. As the day came to a close, they sat on couches and made plans for the weekend sky show at Jules' place. Half an hour later, a rapid sound of footsteps came from above.

"Dad, it's up 600 percent!" The boy was right with the program. He had followed RRL's updates. Another lesson he needed was about discretion, but it made little difference then. Salien ran upstairs after his son, with friends right behind him.

It was true. RRL was up over 600 percent. Without waiting to see which way the price was headed, he reached for the keyboard and trembled with excitement as he typed in a sell order. Subsequent moments dragged out. Would the sale go through? Time stood still as the order's fate lay in someone else's hands. A few seconds seemed like forever.

A new message appeared on the screen… Salien sat back with his eyes closed.

The weekend sky show attracted a huge audience throughout the hemisphere. Thirty people went to Jules' large suburban house to watch, gathered in the sandy backyard. At sunset, ribbons of brilliant purple, green and silver expanded in the north. Colors grew more intense, dancing and flickering like a flood across the sky. The atmospheric administration had put on an aurora for public's enjoyment—one of the most beautiful displays in nature made available on Mars by human ingenuity.

Some guests lay in lounge chairs, some on blankets and others on the sand, looking upward. The show was captivating. One could have stayed for hours just to watch these colors dance.

Salien lay flat on the ground to avoid a sore neck. Vaguely, in the back of his mind, were lingering thoughts of victory from a few days ago. He remembered his charts, calendars and printouts of his trades spread across the room, which read like an indictment. He recalled the surprised look on his guests' faces when they realized what he was doing. They shouldn't have invaded his privacy in the first place, but it made no difference. Far from being made an outcast, he became somewhat of a hero to his friends.

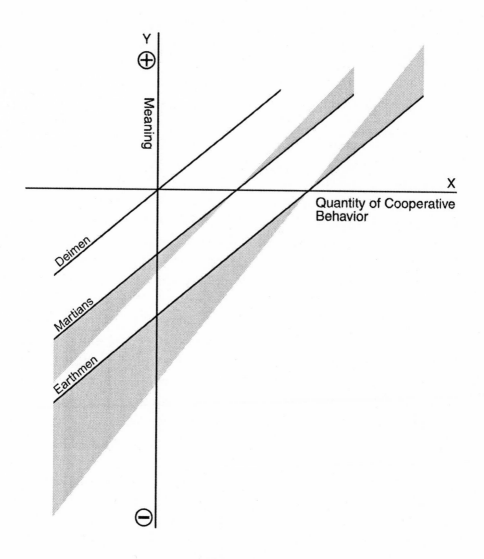

FIG. 9.

EVERY SOCIETY EXISTS IN A GOLDEN MIDDLE OF ITS own—flanked by uninhibited barbarians on its left and by restrictive, overbearing snobs on its right (right and left here and throughout the text refer purely to behavior interpretation within the three-dimensional model, not to political notions of right and left). A culture's line of interpretation during any given time period is influenced by multiple factors—most importantly its ancestry, the environment, and other neighboring societies. Behavior with its cultural interpretation is transmitted both vertically and horizontally. In environmental conditions of relatively abundant resources, low population density, and reduced competition, left shift predominates over time. In environments with high population density, where prolonged competition over resources is present, right shift prevails.

Having come from a relatively competitive, right-shifted ancestry, the Martians now found themselves in a low-population-density, high-resource environment that allows for, and probably favors, left-shifted behavior patterns.

The environment becomes less demanding. An upward redistribution occurs reversing the previously described process. As a line of interpretation moves leftward, behaviors acquire progressively lower negative values on the Y-axis. In other words, the society assigns a more positive meaning to all behaviors, ranging from most destructive through neutral to the most cooperative. Conduct that provokes severe reaction in right-shifted environments (ostracism, exclusion, or worse) becomes merely something at which to laugh or ignore. Negative blocks are gradually removed and third-dimensional behaviors disappear.

In cultural settings where there are few or no dangerous elements to hide from or conspire against, it makes little sense to have secret associations or conspiracies. Organizations that once thrived on exclusion and covert cooperation become unnecessary. They are dissolved or develop into open institutions. Essentially, the four steps of right shift are reversed as a culture becomes left-minded and flat. Martians, who superceded Deimen as the dominant society on the planet, were now themselves becoming Deimen.

It is difficult to classify people as being purely right or left oriented, or to neatly plot each action as a precise point along someone's line of behavior interpretation. Rather, the three-dimensional model represents a sum of our actions over time. Individuals or groups can change depending on cultural surroundings, environmental demands, etc. They may exhibit left-shifted, flat behavior modes; right-shifted, flat modes; right-shifted, indirect/covert modes; or, rarely, left-shifted indirect/covert modes. The fundamental trend, however, is one of moving from left-shifted, flat modes toward right-shifted indirect/covert modes in competitive, densely populated environments and vice versa in low-population, resource-rich environments.

Jules' personality has a relatively right-shifted interpretation line and flat behavior. He interprets the waiter's absence of communication as being very negative and reacts to it in an open and direct manner, staying within the X-Y plane. Salien, on the other hand, more correctly interprets the behavior as being neutral and remains calm in that situation. Jules' mentality is close to Deimen because his behavior is flat (open and direct). He needs only an upward redistribution of interpretation to become one of the Deimen himself. Salien recognizes this trait in his friend and he believes it to be more benign than an indirect, covert personality.

The scene with three men fighting in the club is something most everyone has observed at some point in life. Interpretation of such events is variable. Right-shifted individuals and groups assign a large negative meaning to them, while others take them lightly. The crowd at the club correctly interpreted this fight as a minor event, undeserving of any particular concern. The three men themselves saw it as something insignificant since they returned to neutrality shortly after their dispute. By contrast, a verbal confrontation accompanied by physical contact between right-shifted people would have indicated far greater hostility and would have likely been followed by much third-dimensional behavior in the form of gossip, phone calls, lawsuits, restraining orders, and other actions against the opponents. Such behavior could last for months or even years. The supervisor, being a rightward-oriented individual, saw a great negative meaning in their conflict and took the situation very seriously, following it up based on his own view. This secondary action of assigning a large negative meaning to relatively small quantities of negative behavior causes a downward distribution of interpretation—a key component in cultural right shift.

As a final concept in the analysis, Salien and Jules can be described as being integral parts of our own personalities—one pushes our interpretation to the right—strives for restrictive perfection, demands great cooperation, and punishes small mistakes; the other pushes our line leftward, tolerates negative behavior, and accepts the absence of cooperation. In areas with low population density and abundant resources, Salien predominates, while in competitive, densely populated environments Jules does. Neither can ever prevail completely because the spectrum of behaviors and their interpretation is unlimited.

A CLASH OF CULTURES

S<small>YREMENE CONQUERORS TOOK THE SUBCONTINENT, OVERPOWERING</small> adjacent tribes and nations one by one. Lightning cavalry charges were combined with artillery strikes to bring ill-coordinated opponents quickly and efficiently to their knees.

Their policy toward defeated enemies was simple—whoever offered resistance was put to the sword; others were taken as servants or otherwise integrated into a vast nation.

Time period of Tasainen Khan's reign saw a continued advance of Syremene military, which culminated in its crowning achievement—conquest of the teardrop peninsula and adjacent islands that formed the subcontinent's tail end. The geographic extreme was difficult to penetrate because heavy defenses along a narrow land strip prevented attacking forces from engaging effectively. It created a thirty-year standoff, finally broken by a war of attrition.

Upon entry into the new territories, Khan's soldiers looted the islanders' treasury and publicly executed their most vocal opponents. Brutal as it was, the conduct actually became a liberal arrangement by standards of the time. Recognizing the sensitive nature of the peninsula's and islands' ethnic group, Syremene leadership made a conscious effort to restrain their actions as they tried to integrate these people into the empire. In exchange for subordination to Khan's authority, islanders were allowed to keep most of the original institutions, their language, and places of worship. For their part, local inhabitants accepted the occupation without much protest. Overwhelming majority showed restraint and a great deal of cooperation with the invading force by accepting new institutions imposed upon them and by quickly becoming productive, tribute-paying subjects.

Subsequent decades saw a gradual departure of most occupation troops—only a nominal presence remained. Large segments of civilian population from the mainland stayed on—including many employees of bureaucratic institutions and trade organizations whose fundamental purpose was to ensure a smooth flow of resources and manufactured goods between the territories. Cultural and religious conversion became a secondary goal, which never made significant inroads among native islanders.

Jana, a fourth generation Syremene, lived on the largest island with her husband, two children, and father. They represented a shrinking minority, but had no intentions to leave despite economic hardships and social pressures. In the midst of upheaval with uncertain politics, Jana took a secretarial job in a trading company to support her family through her husband's mysterious illness. He had been unable to work for two weeks and grew weaker each day.

Jana hurried out of her house to go to work on a usual, dreary day. Walking in both directions were dozens of pedestrians. Some carried open umbrellas while others ignored the drizzle. She approached the office building and kept an eye out for demonstrators, but did not see any. Somewhat relieved, she went up the steps and entered the building with a few minutes to spare. Her sister Xenia was already busy at her desk. She wore a new, navy-blue dress in anxious anticipation of a promotion to a management position. Jana wished her good luck in passing.

Early hours went by quickly with on-the-job training. Just before noon, after Xenia's interview with the company president, the sisters met again. A subtle change in her mood alerted Jana to an uncertain outcome.

"How did it go?"

"Pretty well, I suppose. He gave me a lot of compliments, but I never know what he's really thinking unless I hear it from someone else, sometimes not even then. I really wish we had Andis back."

"Too bad he blew it so openly."

It was a reference to the removal of the old president on accusations of embezzlement—the latest in a series of Syremene bureaucrats to be dismissed on one charge or another ranging from theft to issues of morality and personal indiscretions.

Xenia continued, "With the new people, you're constantly pressed to perform. Make on mistake and…"

"I know. Most of it's behind your back."

"They're quite sincere about it, too. That's the scary part. Supposedly, he'll let me know next week."

The sisters stayed together awhile longer before they returned to work. Jana remained at her desk late, until her duties were finished, then started back home. She took the same path, now striated by long afternoon shadows. From a few blocks away, her father could be seen on the balcony holding a tray full of seeds, surrounded by a dozen, or so, pigeons. A widowed pensioner with little real authority to claim, he devoted a great deal of time to caring for the birds and kept order among them, protecting the timid and weak from the aggressors. Upstairs, the old man opened the door and began with an update on his son-in-law's condition.

"Oliver's fever is up to forty. He hasn't been up all day."

Jana sighed and took off her coat. "We better take him to the hospital again."

She slowly approached her husband's room, listening for any sounds. The door was ajar. She leaned against it and pushed it open to find him in bed, covered with a thin sheet. He looked dry and lay motionless, eyes focused on the ceiling. She picked up a cloth, poured water on it, and ran it across his cheeks and forehead.

"How do you feel now?" she asked.

"About the same as yesterday," he said

"Your temperature is higher. Maybe the doctors should see you one more time."

"I doubt they'll come up with anything new."

"Come on, let's try again for my sake."

He stood up to get dressed. Once tight-fitting pants dangled on him—evidence of how much weight he had lost. Jana went to a neighbor to ask for help. She had some luck. The man offered to give them a ride to the hospital.

As they arrived, a familiar routine awaited them: interviews, examinations, and periods of waiting. The staff was familiar with Oliver's situation. He was taken into the exam room reasonably quickly. A young doctor looked in, turned to pick up the chart, and introduced himself. In his early twenties, Jana guessed. A few years younger and he could have been their son.

She went through the routine, pointing out the details of her husband's symptoms and recited what had been done for him before. After a brief examination, the doctor turned toward the exit. Hoping to squeeze out anything new before he left, Jana spoke up.

"What are those red spots on his feet?"

"It's too early to say. We should know more after a further work-up." He excused himself and went out.

About three hours passed before Oliver was assigned to a room and taken upstairs. At time like this, Jana wished they were native islanders. Although there was no doubt that doctors and nurses were overworked and staff members did their best to accommodate everyone, they just seemed to hustle more when the health of native islanders was in question. Perhaps it was a subconscious ethnic discrimination—something the staff themselves didn't notice. At least she'd been able to speak with a senior physician and gain some information about the diagnosis before leaving the hospital.

The following morning, she was awakened by her father's daily routine. He'd been up since 6 A.M. First he had shaved, then wound up the clocks and rearranged small furniture. Jana went to the kitchen to make breakfast for everyone.

"I see they kept him overnight," her father said.

52

"Yes, they think it's a heart infection. At least we have some idea of what's going on."

"What are they doing for it?"

"Antibiotic injections every three hours; I hope the treatment turns him around. I'll have to check on him tonight."

The old man sat on a living room sofa, lit up a cigar, and went through the newspaper. He read headlines out loud to himself, hoping to also catch anyone else's attention.

"'Student organizations emerge as a thorn in Syremene leadership's eye.' The paper's gloating over it, too."

"Students will always protest, Dad. You know that."

"It's not the students. It's the islanders and their rebellion." He paused to cough, then he continued, "Listen to this, 'Last mainland garrisons set to depart the islands.'"

"I know. I heard it yesterday. Why don't you come and join us before the food gets cold?"

He left his cigar in the ashtray, strolled over and sat at the table, then poured himself some coffee. Pigeons had gathered outside. As he took out a slice of bread and opened the balcony door to feed them, a stream of people marching toward city center came into view.

"Demonstrators are gathering," he announced. "Better hurry up before you get caught in the crowd."

Jana went out and leaned over the balcony to get a good look. Two columns were making their way toward downtown from separate directions. Some carried signs and many shouted slogans. It was the fifth day of protest against local administrations' refusal to support the mainland nation in its conflict with aggressors who threatened the subcontinent. Crowds loyal to the mainland were taking a strong stand against islanders' cowardly indifference. Each day, protesters threw rocks, cursed, and fought with police and native people. True to themselves, islanders backed down in most situations, preferring to stand by or run when challenged. After successful demonstrations, protesters would gather for drinking parties to boast of their exploits and ridicule their opponents' cowardice. Street crime occurred as common thugs took advantage of the confusion. Some claimed that local authorities inserted their own men among the masses to commit random acts of violence and discredit the movement. There was no question, however, that most violence came from demonstrators themselves, driven by an antagonism towards the other group and encouraged by a diffusion of responsibility in large crowds.

Jana hugged her kids before she left home. Fortunately, their school was very near which made an encounter with hooligans unlikely. She took her usual route to work and found some safety along the way in the company of two coworkers. When they entered the office building, its inside emptiness became obvious. Many employees had chosen to stay home. Xenia was already at her desk, seemingly preoccupied with her work at hand, but it only appeared that way. The sisters looked at each other. Their embarrassment was understood.

With each passing minute, crowds swelled in the street. Their noise grew to deafening proportions. The few employees inside, native islanders mostly, stood at the windows with a reserved look of condemnation. Civilized people exchanged glances and subdued comments—two ethnic groups only yards apart, yet separated by a cultural abyss.

Sounds of shattered windows came from below, mixed with chanting and the resonation of loudspeakers... Then, just as quickly as the volume rose, it subsided. Most protesters had moved off. As a few stragglers walked around, two shots rang out. In the aftermath, a ten-year-old boy lay mortally wounded on the street. This event's significance would be largely missed at the moment.

Discharged early from work, the sisters went out through deserted streets littered with glass and debris, inspecting the damage along the way. Jana reflected on her close encounter with the crowd.

"Good thing we got in before they blocked the doors. I hope we've seen the last of it."

"Me, too... We'll have a problem if that kid dies. You saw their reaction to the shooting." Xenia continued, "Janus was out today. I looked through his desk and you won't believe what I found."

"Go on."

"An order for sports and hunting ammunition from a supplier I've never heard of, for steel-coated lead bullets—two and a half million rounds."

"My God! How much game does this island have?"

"Exactly my thought... I could report it, but to whom?"

Jana paused for a few moments, then said, "I think you should ignore it. It probably *is* just sports ammunition."

It was clear that she herself hardly believed the last statement, but chose to think so, hoping for a chance it could be true. What could they do anyway? To draw attention to it might bring on a loss of employment, or even worse...

The mostly empty boulevard led straight toward the medical center. Near its entrance, they were stopped briefly at a newly placed security checkpoint before being allowed to proceed upstairs to the third floor.

Oliver greeted them in the hallway, wearing a set of striped pajamas. Although still pale and emaciated, he looked cheery. Penicillin injections had taken effect.

Jana approached and gave him a hug. "You look so much better today, thank God. Your fever has gone away."

"I'm all right, but they told me that injections will go on for three weeks."

He was aware that a less painful method of intravenous infusion was available, but it was technically more difficult to administer and he wasn't the type to demand a different treatment purely for the sake of convenience.

He put on a robe. The three then went out together to sit on a bench. After receiving an injection, Oliver was free for a while and took time to repeat a story from a roommate upstairs who had sold his house in preparation to move away promptly after hospital discharge. The individual considered himself lucky to have found a buyer for the house at half its original value. Property prices had tumbled as many Syremene left their homes, heading what they thought was safer territory.

Oliver thought their reactions bordered on paranoia. He was comfortable on the island and, like his wife, directed most of his scorn toward the protesters. He was greatly embarrassed by earlier events and firmly believed that unrests would subside, as they had before. He respected the local administration for its tempered response to provocations. Islanders he knew showed a great deal of cooperation on a daily basis. All were polite, industrious people—from neighbors and coworkers to hospital staff and others. He was certainly grateful for the level of care devoted to him at the hospital.

They stayed together until after dusk, when a new injection was due. Oliver then headed back upstairs while the sisters took a bus home... With continued treatments, he steadily gained energy. Color gradually returned to his skin. His whole body felt like a pin cushion as injection sites were alternated, but it was a small price to pay for a chance of cure.

Outside, a tense calm pervaded the streets. Demonstrators were no longer seen... In their place came a congregation of islanders. Nearly thirty thousand attended the slain boy's funeral in an orderly procession followed by a candlelight vigil at sunset—local citizens' equivalent of a rambunctious, rock-throwing protest.

The event included a large contingency from the Octagon Association, a little-known, but growing party with a charismatic leadership. Residential lights remained dim through the evening as prominent association members spoke at the funeral to urge restraint in response to the latest crimes, but vow justice for this homicide, condemning the barbarism that caused its perpetration.

From her bedroom window's distance, Xenia observed the procession as it blended with its surroundings and later became a long stream of candlelights. She recognized the dangers of the impending showdown and weighed her options. To move away would mean to give up a career lifestyle—something she could rather easily do, since she was young. Reliance on her own people for support would be futile because they couldn't even help themselves. To remain in her present state was not an option.

She chose to seek safety within the ranks of a new organization for women—the Sisterhood of Octagon—which was dedicated to preserving the islands' culture. Without much delay, Xenia approached a friend from work who was an active participant. Surprisingly, she received assurance of a quick admission. She gained entry after an initiation rite and a swearing-in ceremony, while questions about ethnicity or family background, which would have been easy to figure out, did not come up. Her friend had enough clout to make the acceptance process a mere formality.

Xenia quickly adapted to her niche and found that she could actually identify with the sisterhood's order. She understood the islanders like few of her own people did. Within their often two-faced conduct, they were actually quite sincere and loyal, provided one adhered to some strict rules. Despite its appearance as an ethnocentric organization, in many ways it was a group of inclusion based on behavior. If her own people only knew the right ways... It seemed they weren't bad, just ignorant.

Meanwhile, Jana and kids prepared the apartment for Oliver's return. His three-week ordeal was coming to a close. Likely, a cure had been accomplished. He felt good, clean. On the day of discharge, family members brought presents for the hospital staff and took pictures with them during a nice farewell gathering attended by most employees on the ward.

Later, a number of friends joined Oliver's family for a homecoming party. Their apartment looked very bright, like the first time they moved in. Carpets on the living room floor and hallways that led into bedrooms were freshly cleaned. The place was jammed with people, young and old. As guests settled down, conversations turned to politics and the conflict with the islanders. One salient feature that stood out in people's minds was noise from the demonstrations—the loud slogans.

Each guest shared a unique personal experience connected with recent unrests. Some voiced concern over rumors of deportation, saying that a number of ships were prepared for a large-scale transport to mainland; second-hand news that provided a good topic of conversation and caused some bluster, but little real action or even worry.

After a long evening of listening to advice and many handshakes, Oliver excused himself and retired to his bedroom.

Xenia arrived later, after most people had left. She hadn't come to terms with herself, burdened with dual loyalties. She pulled her sister into the kitchen and tried to convince her to sell the apartment, but once again, she was met with apathy. Doing nothing was the easy way out.

Through subsequent days, everyone followed the events closely. A fragile balance of power had been upset—lower continent faced an invasion similar to Khan's conquest generations earlier, but this time, Syremenes were forced to give way. Weekend news brought discouraging reports from the mainland front... As the reality of war drew near, many original hawks—particularly among students—began to appreciate the island's isolation.

Oliver was looking forward to a return to work. As he lay awake on a Monday before dawn, a loud, rapid banging on the front door startled him and awakened everyone inside. He rose to open the door. In no time, regular police and the Octagon Guard swarmed into their apartment.

Oliver was stunned by a realization that rumors were true. He felt betrayed. The civilized, industrious people he knew, the ones who had saved his life, would now deport him.

While they hurriedly dressed, Jana pleaded to be allowed to carry out some belongings. Her request was refused. Out on the street, along with several neighbors and kids by her side, she found an officer of the Octagon Guard and approached him.

"Can you at least let us bring out some clothes?"

"Don't worry about them. You will be taken care of," he answered. "Move on." There was something sinister about his smile.

Vehicles loaded with people made their way to the outskirts of town and beyond—northward, toward the old docks; more accurately—the cliffs that lined the bay on one side. This area had been deserted for years. Moss and weeds grew between cracks in the asphalt.

A huge crowd waited at the stairway gate in preparation to board the ships. As more people arrived by the minute, outer edge of the mass pressed against a thin metal rail never made to hold back more than a few visitors. A young woman with two kids of her own turned and spoke out: "They're out of their minds. Look how steep that stairway is…must be a hundred-foot drop beneath it."

As new arrivals gathered behind her, Jana moved sideways and cleared some space for her children. The presence of an ambulance was reassuring.

The mass, which grew to several thousand by noontime, became restless. Many urged for the gate to be opened, while some derided the soldiers… Others begged for personal needs. Sun's energy was now mercilessly beaming down on them. Surrounded by men and women, Jana raised herself on her toes to look around. She couldn't see the ambulance any more.

A military convoy, mostly trucks, approached from the south. Vehicles slowed and pulled up alongside the people, then turned ninety degrees to face away from them. Two by two, soldiers leaped out; tight-fitting ashen uniforms emblazoned with orange octagons. Jana had difficultly seeing more than that and turned to her husband, who was almost a foot taller, to check for any signs. He had a strange look on his face. She remembered their times together. Scenes from their marriage flashed through her mind in rapid succession, but she couldn't recall ever seeing this look—not even during his illness. She straightened up and drew in a deep breath as if to ask a question; but then she stopped and held still… There was no need. In the last moments of her life, everything had become clear.

Suddenly, gentlemen officers of the Octagon Guard turned into raging madmen and screamed out orders to fire. A loud gasp went up as the first salvo hit the crowd. Between the bodies and the flying elbows, Jana caught sight of machine gun fire from the back of a truck and threw herself on top of her kids.

Meanwhile, back in town, from the relative safety of her new status, Xenia suspected what she would learn about years later. She stood alongside the Sisters of Octagon and prayed—for a return of Syremene nation.

KHAN'S BUREAUCRACY INTEGRATED THE ENTIRE SUBCONTINENT into its society, except the population of the peninsula and adjacent islands, despite making very liberal coexistence arrangements. What happened?

This population's unique nature lies largely in its right-shifted interpretation and behavior patterns. The quantity of cooperative behavior it would have taken to establish a positive relationship with residents of the peninsula and islands far exceeded what Syremene culture would or could offer. It certainly exceeded requirements from other conquered populations on the subcontinent. On the other hand, negative events that would have been taken lightly on mainland (the war, execution of vocal opponents, looting the treasury, etc.) carried an enormous hostile interpretation among islanders, which lasted over decades, even generations. Persistent uncooperative behavior and overt hostile demonstrations from immigrant groups ensured the continuation of a very negative relationship.

It's important to emphasize variabilities in the perception of negative actions. Demonstrators and other immigrants meant to express antagonism, but the meaning perceived by islanders far exceeded the intended meaning. Extensive third-dimensional behaviors that existed within the island's right-shifted culture provided for indirect and cover responses to the hostility—collaboration with outside forces, removal of opposition bureaucrats using indirect tactics, secret acquisition of weapons, planning various actions against the other group, etc. The ruse lasted to the end with most intended victims oblivious to hidden activity until its final act, when they became an inseparable part of it.

Geographic extremes such as land narrows, peninsulas, and islands tend to run out of space and resources relatively quickly, which leads to early, intense competition and right-shifted (hypersensitive-indirect/covert) behavior patterns greatly exceeding those on adjacent mainland. Spectacular culture clashes of the kind described here can develop.

Left-shifted cultures frequently tend to see rightward-oriented behavior as weakness or cowardice. Absence of an open, direct response to provocations is seen as an inability to respond. In reality, the response is very often merely displaced away from public scene by a cultural negative block. Challengers will often be amused and will threaten, provoke, and attack their opponents to test the limits of "cowardice," completely unaware about the hostility provoked, along with reprisals from third dimension.

History abounds with astounding examples of inhumanity committed by very enlightened cultures. People have wondered how can societies so civilized, cooperative, and industrious engage in behavior so malicious.

Perhaps you have know two people, one of whom smiles, cooperates, gives out compliments, and does everything right, while the other, lacking in social graces, acts rudely, ignores others, and argues. Yet, somehow you feel the crude individual, being straightforward, is actually better than the polite person. It's not your imagination. This apparent paradox may be explained by the three-dimensional model.

As illustrated in Figure 10, an increasing cultural right shift will lead to larger and larger quantities of cooperative behavior necessary to maintain neutral relationships. Those same lines of interpretation, extended down the Y-axis, lead to progressively greater hostility toward an absence of cooperation and negative behavior; therefore, the more polite and cooperative people become in maintaining daily relationships, the more intolerant and hostile they become toward others! The two are actually linked by common lines of interpretation. See Figure 10.

A typical sequence of events occurs when a right-shifted person or group shows extensive cooperation and positive communication in trying to maintain a relationship. If the other party does not respond with adequate cooperation, a hostile relationship is established (with level of hostility proportional to the right shift). A negative block prevents an open, direct response to offending absence of cooperation. Subsequent hostility becomes displaced into the third dimension as an indirect or covert negative behavior—a stab in the back.

The association of increasing quantities of publicly or directly displayed cooperative behavior with increasing quantities of indirect or covert hostile behavior can be called bimodal behavior or *bimodal increment*.

In her conversations, Xenia correctly identifies a sincere quality to the two-faced behavior around her. How can two-faced or bimodal behavior be sincere? It can be if it's a part of a single behavior interpretation chi (bix). A culture's line of interpretation, along with its lines of direct (open) and indirect (covert) behavior, form an X, which can be called the behavior-interpretation chi (bix), illustrated in Figure 11. People can think and behave in a straightforward manner along a single right-shifted line and react accordingly, sticking to a corresponding third dimension line without breaking rules. A cultural negative block prevents direct hostile behavior and the antagonism is honestly performed in an indirect or covert manner.

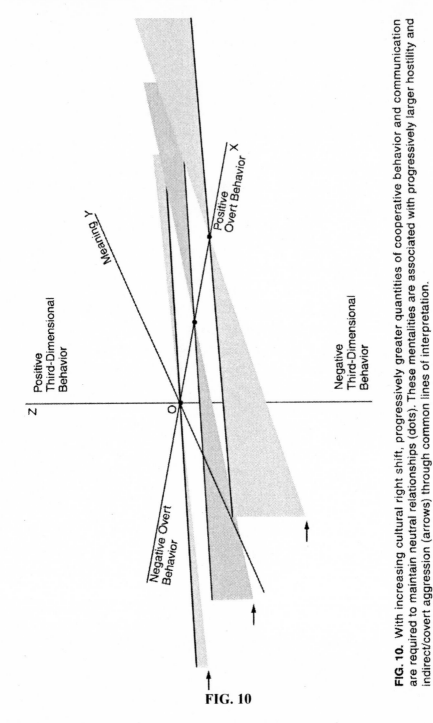

FIG. 10

FIG. 10. With increasing cultural right shift, progressively greater quantities of cooperative behavior and communication are required to maintain neutral relationships (dots). These mentalities are associated with progressively larger hostility and indirect/covert aggression (arrows) through common lines of interpretation.

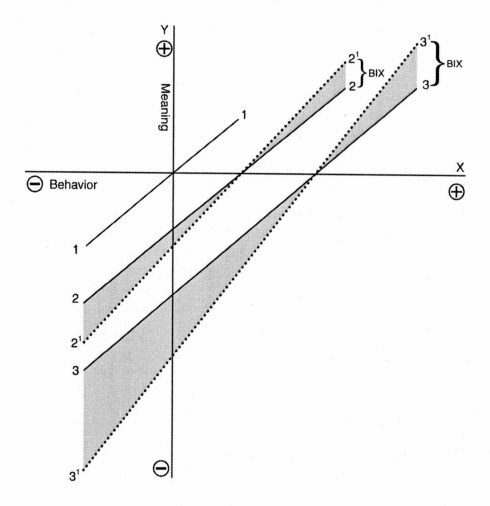

FIG. 11.

Straightforward behavior, however, does not explain all factors that can contribute to inter-group conflict. A breakdown of relationship is a major driving force behind collective actions. When a number of interactions take place outside of the expected bix, due to either cultural differences or abnormal or immoderate behavior, relationship breakdowns can occur. In such situations, left-shifted groups tend to gravitate toward extreme forms of second-dimension behavior (open, direct hostility) while right-shifted groups engage in very negative indirect and covert behaviors. Common examples of cultural miscommunication that could lead to relationship breakdown include:

1. Right-shifted people who observe open, direct negative behavior coming from a left-shifted culture assign a disproportionately large negative meaning to the behavior and attribute it to an irrational frame of mind.
2. Left-shifted people who observe indirect, covert or bimodal behavior believe it's a malicious two-faced action without rules or reason.

Many such miscommunications over time can lead to prolonged or chronic breakdowns of relationships in which immoderate actions without rules or reason *do* become the standard interactive conduct.

With regard to organized public displays of protest: In a right-shifted society, an orderly procession represents the *second dimension equivalent* to a loud, rock-throwing protest in left-shifted cultures (Fig. 12). Due to the presence of a cultural negative block, the most extreme public display of hostility in local islanders' society is a reserved, low-toned assembly. More extensive hostile actions are displaced into the third dimension and are turned into behaviors such as collaboration with outside parties, secret procurement of weapons, secluded preparation for war, etc. With a further cultural right shift, a society may dispense with overt signs of hostility altogether and proceed straight to extensive covert actions without any warning.

By executing vocal opponents on the island, original Syremene invaders introduced a negative block, sparing those islanders who remained quiet and expressed hostility in indirect and covert ways. Later, segments of immigrant minority that survived included people whose interpretation was rightward enough to assign a large negative meaning to small warning signs and react accordingly (sell their property and leave). Among them was Xenia, who joined the Sisterhood of Octagon for the same reason. Therefore, prolonged conflict between two groups ultimately produced a natural selection in favor of right-shifted people on both sides.

Oliver's surprise over islanders' final actions against him can be explained by his lack of understanding of their mentality. What he observed from the islanders was mostly the quantity of cooperative behavior necessary to maintain neutral relationships, which he mistakenly believed to be friendship (Fig. 12). Islanders' attitudes toward him weren't nearly as positive as he thought despite the overt politeness, the cooperation shown, and the procedures that initially saved his life.

As a final point in the analysis, Jana's perceived lack of effort from hospital's staff, the "subconscious discrimination," represents an interesting phenomenon based within the three-dimensional model. Immigrants, who are a left-shifted group, make negative statements with a comparatively small negative meaning. Hospital staff learns from experience to pay more attention to the same complaints (negative statements) from right-shifted patients because they carry a greater negative meaning. Observed differences in responses to the same symptoms and complaints from various groups are, therefore, real, but have little to do with ethnic discrimination and more to do with behavior interpretation.

Modern health-care institutions nationwide and around the world have made great efforts to create fair, uniform patient management without regard to race, ethnicity, gender, etc. They have been very successful in doing so. Various groups, however, fall along different lines of interpretation within the three-dimensional model and sometimes tend to be managed differently for identical complaints, which probably accounts for much of the perceived bias.

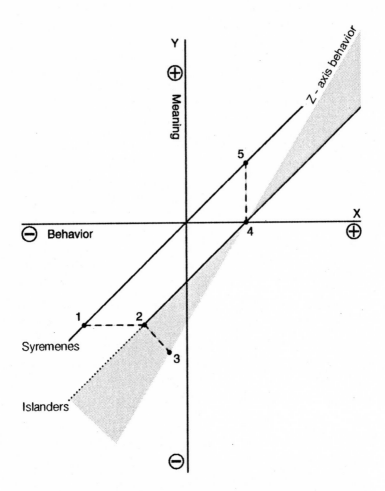

FIG. 12. A loud, rock-throwing protest (1) in a left-shifted culture is the negative-relationship-defining equivalent of an orderly procession in a right-shifted society (2). More extensive forms of hostility in the island's society are displaced into the third dimension (3) and become indirect collaboration with outside parties, covert acquisition of weapons, etc.

Most of the islanders' behavior toward Oliver (4) was the quantity of cooperation necessary to maintain neutral relationships. Based on his left-shifted interpretation, he mistakenly believed it meant friendship (5).

A COACH AGAINST THE RIGHT SHIFT

J.D. WAS A BASKETBALL PLAYER, DECORATED ARMY VETERAN AND a pillar of the community.

After an honorable discharge from the service, he resumed a career in basketball as a player and later turned to coaching. With an energetic and inspiring personality, he became the head coach of a nationally recognized team by his late thirties. At the onset, he hired two former associates with proven flexibility and communication skills to serve as assistants and set out to build the most winning period in the club's history.

J.D. imposed his agenda in a way that few colleagues at the game's top levels could do. The key to success was a blend of discipline acquired in the military with a flexibility that took into account each player's traits. This strategy produced an unprecedented win-loss ratio over a decade and half. It brought fame and recognition to his rural home town along with two championship trophies.

The coach had a reputation for caring about his players beyond confines of the basketball court. He inquired about their home life and helped with social and financial adjustments, particularly in cases of young recruits from low-income families. He spent long hours on the phone making sure his players stayed on track and regularly invited them home for dinner. In one instance, a new recruit received substantial help from him during a family emergency—a gesture that was well remembered. He would remain the coach's friend for life.

Well into the second decade of coaching, regular seasons were marked by outstanding play. J.D. and the team looked forward to playoffs, ranked third in the league with a good shot at winning the championship. They breezed through to the semifinals game and expected another victory. At halftime, their lead was 51-43. The game continued into the second half at a similar pace. The lead was extended by two points, but then the team managed to be outscored twenty to eight in final minutes. One free throw narrowed the score to 91-90. On a turnover, J.D.'s team took their last time-out. Inbound pass went to the center, who took a jump shot at the buzzer—and missed.

It was a difficult loss to swallow. As J.D. walked toward interview room, he refused to shake hands with the opposing coach. In fact, he went past him without even a nod or a glance. During previous seasons, he had done what is known as a blow-by in coaching—quick handshakes without conversation that indicated some disrespect. He had also ignored people outright, but this incident evoked a lot of controversy. Public's reaction forced him to make a televised speech that included a statement of apology. To make his case, J.D. cited prior affronts performed by other coaches—insults and blow-bys. He pointed out that his own conduct was in proportion to that of other people's and indicated he had been unfairly singled out. The apology was accepted and the controversy gradually subsided.

Next several seasons brought mixed results on the court—alternating winning and losing records. The staff meticulously studied films to make defensive adjustments before each game. They carefully reviewed upcoming opponents' moves to make sure each player had a well-rehearsed game plan. Particular attention was paid to rebounding at both ends. With a traditionally high-scoring team, work on improvements in defense promised to yield greatest results. Their plans paid off and the team reached finals once again. During the championship game, they took a commanding 18-6 lead at the onset. Several lay-ups, jump shots, and difficult long distance attempts resulted in scores. It seemed as if everything a player tossed up went in. At the other end, team's defensive adjustments threw their opponents out of sync. By halftime, J.D. could sense a victory at hand. His old confidence had returned. Fortunate trends continued into the second half—with a high percentage of field goals made, their lead was maintained at 10 to 15 points into the last minutes. The feeling was exhilarating. It was a time span one could freeze for a week. J.D. had a third championship under his belt and he became a legend. He enjoyed the celebrations and sat on his laurels for most of the short summer.

In the years ahead, J.D.'s teams would excel during regular seasons only to be knocked out by lower-ranked opponents during playoffs. The game became more physical all around, especially at its top levels. Film analysis became an increasingly sophisticated science. J.D. looked for new ways to improve efficiency. Assistant coaches and the trainer introduced a weightlifting regimen for softer players. After film reviews, one player or another would be regularly singled out for criticism to cut down on their mistakes. The coach became aware that conversations, interviews and endless handshakes interfered with performance and drained precious time and energy. He wasn't becoming any younger either. He made a conscious effort to minimize interactions with friends, as well as former players and the public, in order to devote more attention to coaching. This would undoubtedly offend people, but a decision had to be made to sacrifice some public relations for the sake of performance.

The autumn after their championship season began with a lingering fatigue. Still, victories continued as players led by a strong center took several games by an average margin of only three points. A rematch of the previous year's finals came early in regular season. In an intense and close contest, the lead changed hands frequently. Score was tied with four minutes left. Then, J.D.'s forward faked a jump shot and drove in for a lay-up as a whistle blew to end the play. The bench went up, expecting a free throw, but this play was called back on a charging violation. J.D. went ballistic in a second. Since he watched the guard's feet through the entire sequence, he couldn't have disagreed more… The coach ran out, yelled at the referee, and promptly earned a technical foul, which did not seem to faze him much. His tirade continued as he walked back toward the bench. He cursed several times and kicked a chair into the stands, narrowly missing a VIP spectator in the front row. A second technical foul was called and J.D. was thrown out of the game. Despite this episode, his team rallied and won by a comfortable margin.

While the coach had support from local fans, media's reaction grew, as did community leaders' condemnations. Some reactions included calls for his dismissal. This incident was analyzed and reanalyzed. J.D.'s other shenanigans came into spotlight as experts vied to explain the causes of such behavior. He became labeled as the bad boy of coaching and a poor role model for younger generations. A trend of public gaffes developed, followed by apologies and promises of improvement.

Feeling a pressure to change his image, J.D. started to wear elegant suits. He changed his hairstyle to conform to a more modern look. Summer vacation was filled with charitable events—an activity he spearheaded with genuine enthusiasm. Staff members and assistant coaches felt the society had an excellent capacity for forgiveness, which turned out to be right. Controversies gradually faded and J.D. focused his attention back on the game.

Subsequent generation of players was blessed with a young leader on the court—a talented forward who possessed a great ability to anticipate. The fresh recruit had a mental picture of the court like few other players. It was a difficult quality to teach. He predicted his teammates' and opponents' moves like a good chess player, as he kept track of where the momentum would carry everyone. This skill ensured accurate passing. The offense improved on records from previous high-scoring seasons. Young stars reached quarterfinals twice in a row. Although a championship eluded them, their style of play earned them wide respect. The ability to maintain a winning record so consistently was, in itself, a proof of greatness.

Personality quirks notwithstanding, J.D. retained a solid following among fans, who took his actions in stride. He correctly believed the public would look at the overall picture of his accomplishments in a positive light.

The next turning point came in a mundane regular season game. J.D.'s guard had sulked for most of the first half and missed several jump shots. He lost the ball on a bad pass, which was understandable, but then he made a turnover and committed a foul. J.D. sent in a replacement and told the removed player exactly what he thought about his performance. He got into the man's face—at one point, as the player tried to stand up, his coach grabbed his shirt to yank him back into the seat.

A reaction was once again in the making. Amid this new controversy, J.D. refused an invitation to attend a gala dinner sponsored by the club's administration and chose to go fishing instead. When questioned about the snub, he brought up health issues and explained how such events caused him severe heartburn...poor man! Here, reflux sufferers and others could feel sympathy for the ailing hero. He hadn't told anyone about his esophageal affliction and remained secluded to bear the pain in silence. He should have announced his condition long ago. There was nothing to hide. From then on, special dinners would be cooked for him, custom ordered and guaranteed not to cause an acid upsurge. It was the least a town could do for its favorite star.

But graces vanished when the veteran revealed the cause of his inside pains: "The food isn't giving me a heartburn; it's the assholes I have to sit with!"

That was it! Vile language aimed at foremost citizens was the last straw. Controversial behavior was televised and a hunt was on.

Once again, the coach played defense off court. Behavior experts and talk show hosts examined the events. During TV

interviews, questions came up about J.D.'s upbringing—
reported physical abuse by his father, post-traumatic stress
disorder related to military service, and other issues, real and
imagined.   Reactions to events were deeper than ever.
Accusations of arrogance resurfaced.   Tapes of blow-bys were
shown accompanied by commentary that, J.D. thought, would
have made a saint look guilty.   He asked his audiences not to
blow his actions out of proportion—as he pointed out the
difficulties of keeping up great records in addition to a perfect
image off court. He argued that after so many long, exhausting
seasons, one should have the leeway to act out occasionally. To
demonstrate the difficulties imposed by constant demands for
cooperation, he went out into the audience, giving compliments
to participants and asked about their health and family.   With
theatrical exaggeration, he described what he called "the
absurdity of excessive politeness." It took up ten minutes of the
show and in itself became a disputed topic.

Fortune smiled on the coach one more time as the prevailing
mood of forgiveness outweighed the sanctions. He was slapped
with a ten-game suspension. Players made a special effort to fill
the void. They did a good job and won seven out of ten games.
The team continued to perform well despite adversity.   On the
court and away, players weren't any more immune to
controversy than their coach, but it wouldn't present a
significant obstacle. Gradually, they would learn to pay careful
attention to words and actions, in proportion to their celebrity
status—the same way J.D. had learned, if somewhat belatedly.

Injuries prevented any major advance in the next three
seasons; however, the following year, J.D. and company outdid
everyone's expectations and reached the championship game. In
a contest against stronger opponents—behind during final
minutes—the coach put together all of his enthusiasm to give an
intense, yet level-headed speech. His men responded. First a
jump shot went in, then a lay-up. They forced a turnover and
rallied to hit eight unanswered shots. This time, they would

hang on to win. It would be widely held as the greatest come-from-behind championship in decades.

Michael Pak, M.D.

SEVERAL ADVERSE FACTORS MARRED AN OTHERWISE BRILLIANT coaching career. Among the many forces that influenced J.D.'s behavior may have been his upbringing (parental conduct), post-traumatic stress disorder, and personal difficulty with temper control. Also, the sheer volume of interactions over many seasons increases the likelihood of controversial negative events. However, additional important phenomena at play are society's decreasing acceptance of negative behavior as a part of cultural right shift and the coach's interaction with situations and people more right-shifted than himself. While this behavior had not changed very much over the years, the society's attitude had.

By ignoring his opponent after the semifinals game, J.D. meant to make a negative statement, but the level of hostility perceived was far greater than he intended. Reactions from onlookers were also more severe than he expected due to behavioral right shift.

Blow-bys are a good example of a cooperative behavior that defines a negative relationship. The person doing a blow-by engages in some positive communication and shakes hands, but the quantity, intensity, and/or duration of this behavior is inadequate to establish even a neutral relationship in right-shifted situations. An advance in cultural right shift designates progressively stronger hostile meanings to blow-bys, which leads to intense or prolonged retributions. Among left-shifted people, on the other hand, a blow-by is something neutral. A left-inclined observer tends to think, "What's the big deal?" He or she finds it difficult to understand the hostile reactions around such an event.

Assigning negative relationships to the absence of cooperation can place excessive and sometimes impossible demands on a person (the basketball coach in this case). In a busy situation, it is easy to ignore acquaintances simply because of fatigue or a momentary lapse of attention. This behavior can easily be misinterpreted as hostility and may bring serious consequences to one's reputation and career.

People are often forced to compromise between devoting energy to career goals or public relations. Overall, the coach did a fairly good job as he worked to balance the two.

LYDIA'S PROJECT

THE NEW ASSIGNMENT ON A CORPORATE HEADQUARTERS BUILDING under construction brought her to a close encounter with a technologically advanced, but somewhat naïve group of people who formed most of the project team. Her position as assistant project manager involved close collaboration with native architects and engineers connected with her organization. Her position called for some supervision of men from a patriarchal society, but she was assured the duties wouldn't present a problem at this level. There was every reason to believe in success. Despite cost overruns and delays, feasibility studies indicated the buildings would likely fulfill the investors' objectives as well as remain environmentally friendly. Fitting together all the components of the center within an artistic external design would require close cooperation between project managers, architects, and structural and mechanical engineers.

From a high corridor, Lydia watched the construction under way and the participants who were coming to attend her first presentation in an improvised conference room. The room and the rest of the center looked surreal, almost beautiful. Like so many buildings, it would probably appear better under construction than when finished. Cameras mounted overhead recorded the construction and transmitted live images to a web site.

At 8:15, as the architects, engineers, and consultants continued to walk in, Lydia began her presentation with a chart that outlined the modified design of several wings. Computer-generated forms were based on the cardboard models produced to curb the external extravagance—the newest effort to contain cost overruns, which had already reached 30 percent of the original funding. After thoroughly explaining the outlines featured on two charts, Lydia dimmed the lights and focused on the details presented on a slide. No sooner had she started than Pascal, the senior project manager, asked if she had checked the seismic compliance for proposed modifications.

She responded, "I am not sure I know the local guidelines, but regional procedures are the same and all the modifications conform to…"

Without waiting for her to finish, Pascal retorted, "Your first answer was right. You don't know it." He then went on criticize how the plans just happened to conform, by accident. It was an inconsequential point meant more to prop up his small town ego than the corporate headquarters.

Pascal's remarks pretty much set a tone for the rest of the presentation. Descriptions of slides were followed by cold, stolid reactions from her audience—flat gazes and silence interspersed with occasional jabs and humorous remarks. The workers' attitudes seemed more than demanding. In fact, they were downright unappreciative.

Andrew, a sharp structural engineer sitting in the first row, gave her some hints of positive reinforcement throughout this session. Aside from being agreeable, which complimented his authoritative image, he demonstrated a thorough understanding of the concepts. Lydia would delegate a great deal of responsibility to him in the days to come. She finished her presentation with a description of the visitors' information center, then she packed the equipment and headed out. Andrew helped her carry out some materials.

Her hotel room was a small cubicle with two beds and its lighting was reminiscent of a college dormitory. Taking into account where she was, the accommodations were pretty good.

Lydia spent the next several days shuffling from her room to the offices, making explicit written instructions to reinforce what she had said during meetings. It was difficult to assess how much information went out accurately since associates often ignored her and disassociated from conversations. Communication was a challenge. Other participants weren't very polite amongst themselves, either. Still, Lydia felt singled out to some degree, despite being prepared and positive beyond usual.

Thursday night, a number of friends and relatives gathered for a party, including Pascal's family. Being an informal event, Lydia wore corduroy pants and a blouse—decent enough attire to pass without standing out. She mingled with the guests for about a half hour. Across the room, Pascal was busy gobbling down chicken wings. Lydia sat down beside his wife and sister-in-law, complimented them on the hors d'oeuvres, and asked about their trip. His wife returned a lukewarm greeting with only a few sullen words despite seeming pleasant enough earlier, during their introductions. The sister-in-law remained oblivious, as if in a world of her own. Nonchalantly, she lit a cigarette. Lydia slumped in her chair and guessed at the reasons for the cold reception. Yes, she did have a bad hair day and her outfit wasn't exactly the best she owned, but the other two didn't look all that much better. It was probably Pascal, she thought. What he must have said behind her back could fill volumes.

"Just what I needed," she grumbled inside. Instead of spending the summer on vacation, she was stuck in a dormitory in the middle of nowhere with these...some nerve! Her sophisticated colleagues at home know how to appreciate looks and brains while the bumpkins here just couldn't recognize a good thing if it hit them in the face. She retired to her room early to read through magazines before going to bed.

The subsequent day, Andrew was carrying a set of prints from his car when Lydia met him with a smile.

"It seems you've been busy. I missed you at the party last night," she said.

"Thanks, I wish I had gone."

"I'd like to see those if you don't mind."

"Sure. I am glad I was able to finish on time."

Andrew followed her to the office and stood at her side while she reviewed the outlines in preparation for a proposal to reduce the F wing. His plan was bold, even if only theoretical, to relieve some complicated hoisting procedures. He conceived the idea before the meetings, but he felt it was too radical to discuss openly. It looked good on paper—somewhat different.

Lydia liked the idea very much. They took a tour outside, inspecting this venue from different angels and conjured up images from the standpoint of a visitor who would walk into the plaza for the first time. As they lingered in the light breeze, she thanked him for all the help.

Their next move would be to run the plans by Pascal before a new meeting to present the modifications could take place. Lydia turned on her heel and started inside, handing the prints to Andrew. Back at the office, the door shut behind them. She leaned against the edge of the desk and dialed upstairs.

"Help yourself to a coffee," she said and motioned for Andrew to take a seat. He merely laid the prints down.

The line was busy. As she hung up the phone and looked out the window, Andrew approached her from the side, took her hand and began to embrace her, whispering how much he had hoped for a sign from the first day.

Startled, she pulled away. "No, I didn't mean to..." She staggered backwards, moved around the furniture, and quickly regained her composure. "I am sorry. Not now."

Andrew stood for a few moments, apologized and started to go out, but then stopped at the door. He turned toward the desk again, looking grim.

Tension grew. He approached slowly, deliberately—to pick up the prints. Then, he went out for good.

The next morning, Lydia woke up early from a vivid dream, with thoughts about the encounter. She dressed and went for a quick breakfast and a briefing with the senior project manager. Afterward, she circles the offices once. Andrew was conspicuously absent.

The scheduled conference took place before noon, partially at Lydia's insistence. It was a time when everyone's attention was high and the participants tended to be prompt and efficient. Andrew was in the hallway parting with a consultant when she approached. She spoke right away, from a distance.

"I hope you had enough time to prepare."

"I think so. Pascal will do most of the talking anyway."

She breathed a sigh of relief and continued, "About yesterday... You have to understand—it was unexpected. Will you join me for a drink afterwards?"

He smiled at the words and nodded, remembering, "Not now."

Lydia was an experience architect whose creativity and efficiency earned the respect of intellectuals. Here, during the brief span of her assignment, she was ignored, insulted, and subjected to an abrupt sexual advance. Much of the conduct toward her could have been adequate grounds for a lawsuit in a different place. Yes, she adjusted well, chose to forgive, and eventually become engaged to Andrew. She later brought him a cosmopolitan environment for an opportunity to live through some adjustments himself.

SCIENTIFIC KNOWLEDGE AND TECHOLOGICAL ADVANCEMENT ARE not necessarily intertwined with right-shifted frames of mind. Educated professionals can display surprisingly left-shifted behavior modes.

Lydia encountered just such a group on her assignment. From her right-shifted view, an entire spectrum of behaviors was interpreted as far more negative than intended by her hosts. She saw Pascal's rude verbal jabs, accepted locally as something minor, as very hateful insults. The aloof behavior exhibited by Pascal's wife and sister-in-law had a neutral meaning. Lydia, however, took it to mean disdain and immediately looked for causes and accompanying indirect and covert behavior. She thought she found it in the form of gossip about her performance and/or appearance. In a right-shifted context, overtly ignoring someone would probably be connected with extensive forms of negative behavior behind the person's back. These interactions are illustrated in Figure 13.

When negative meaning is assigned to absence of cooperation and communication, the offended person will look for reasons and often mistakenly attribute the event to factors such as performance, appearance, race, title, etc. It is easy to think: "They are ignoring me because I am not as smart, or rich, or good looking" or "...because I am black, white, Asian..." and conjure up all kinds of negative attitudes associated with this lack of communication. In reality, the only reason for the blasé conduct may be that it's their neutral posture and no accompanying hostility exists at all.

Faced with perceived negative attitudes, right-shifted people can become depressed or alienated and lose motivation. Their performance can suffer or become dysfunctional.

Flexibility, on the other hand, is a valuable asset for helping people to transcend behavioral differences. The ability to bridge the gap between lines of interpretation can open up opportunities that would otherwise be missed.

Michael Pak, M.D.

Lydia's initial level of cooperation and positive communication toward Andrew was intended to convey superficial politeness; however, from his perspective, the meaning was much more positive, indicating flirtation. Such interactions certainly occur within the same social environments, but cross-culturally, these events are even more likely because a gap often exists between lines of interpretation. Fortunately, both partners bridged the gap *and* found each other desirable, which produced a happy ending.

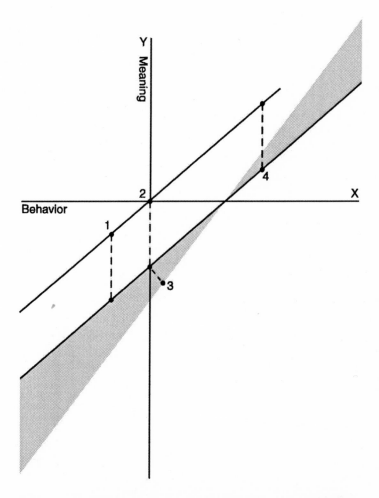

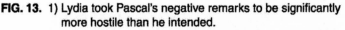

FIG. 13. 1) Lydia took Pascal's negative remarks to be significantly more hostile than he intended.

2) The wife and sister-in-law's absence of positive communication was seen as disdain.

3) Lydia searched for reasons for the perceived negative attitudes and thought she found them—in third dimensional behaviors associated with her own line of interpretation.

4) The initial positive communication shown toward Andrew was superficial politeness, but he saw it as a much stronger positive meaning based on his left-shifted interpretation.

85

CONCLUSION

ANOMIE IS A KEY CONCEPT IN MODERN SOCIOLOGY. ITS ROOTS DATE back more than twenty-five centuries. The literal meaning of anomie is "without law or norms," but a precise definition for the idea has not been established. For some, it represents a breakdown of social structure caused by discrepancy between desired goals and legitimate means of achieving them. For others, it is the absence of restraints on human aspirations. Also included in the definition are conditions of self-to-other alienation and conflicts among belief systems in a society. Differences in observers' personal and professional experience and backgrounds influence how anomie is interpreted. Various definitions are mutually complimentary since an absence of rules in one behavior arena can lead to a relationship breakdown in another.

Anomie, as it relates to the three-dimensional model, can be defined as the breakdown of relationships due to interactive behaviors outside accepted behavior interpretation lines or below the negative block threshold. It can occur among individuals, groups, and entire nations. This type of anomie is likely a major contributor to all forms of anomie that exist within and among societies.

While it is difficult, if not impossible, to predict specific behaviors, since numerous factors come together to produce even a single decision, the three-dimensional model can likely be used with a high degree of certainty to predict the probability of behavior types (cooperative, neutral, hostile, direct, indirect) and their magnitude. It can be very useful when analyzing interactions after the fact.

Michael Pak, M.D.

The principal goal of this work is to graphically outline various behavior and interpretation modes based on cultural background and/or genetic predisposition. My intent is certainly not to label some people as crude or backward because of left-shifted behavior and another population as advanced or sophisticated by virtue of being right-shifted. While most protagonists happen to be left-shifted, the three-dimensional model should not be seen as a means to portray certain people as good or evil based on their interpretation lines. Cultural right shift can be viewed quite favorably as humanity's natural adaptation to specific environments or as a useful mode for ensuring personal and group survival. Many societies that can be described as left-shifted have shown reprehensible human rights records and aggression against neighbors. Other right-oriented groups have demonstrated cooperation, understanding, and sincere tolerance even under attack. People can spend a great deal of time acting out hostilities along a left line or use their life wisely along the positive aspects of right-sided behavior.

The move from caste-based interaction modes in which people are verbally assaulted and even beaten with impunity, to more complicated patterns, while probably accompanied by more surreptitiousness, may be a natural progress. In some ways, heterogeneous societies have no choice but to move right. However, I do believe an element of danger exists in an excessive behavioral right shift because it lowers the threshold for establishing negative relationships.

Recent national statistics have indicated an overall decline in homicide, but an increase in a certain kind of violence—the type that's conducted with elaborate preparation before a final act of shooting. This is consistent with the model's prediction about decreasing hostility conducted along the second dimension and an increase in negative Z-axis behavior with a cultural right shift. An important future task for sociologists, psychologists, and others professionals will be to figure out ways to reduce these covertly-planned hostilities.

As the new century brings an ever-increasing weapons technology, insight into behavior dynamics becomes more crucial to peace and prosperity than ever. Widespread efforts are currently under way to ensure stability in volatile regions.

Peacekeepers continuously hold open aggression at bay and organizations responsible for these efforts deserve all the help they can get. At the top levels of world leadership, theatrical displays of antagonism are constantly being suppressed. Preponderance of our individual and collective work contains mostly sincere intentions toward establishing greater cooperation between societies. These are all positive events that serve to maintain stability.

It is now equally important to prevent a global redistribution of interpretation as well as to reduce the proliferation of hidden activities.

Generations in the late twentieth century enjoyed cultural environments marked by predominantly positive and neutral relationships within most populations. Most leaders have been responsible and cooperative. But leaderships mainly reflect the general populations' conduct. A global redistribution of interpretation, combined with advancing Z-axis class behaviors, may bring about long, covert preparations that culminate in sudden warfare reminiscent of the early twentieth century—this time on an even greater scale. This can and should be prevented. To that effect, I hope that awareness about the three-dimensional model will become an instrument of understanding and peace, since we are all inhabitants of one island equally subjected to its rules.

Michael Pak, M.D.

SUMMARY

INTERACTIVE BEHAVIOR IS A LINEAR PHENOMENON GUIDED BY relationships among people.

Relationships, in turn, are influenced by culturally determined meanings assigned to various behaviors. Each culture assigns values to behaviors, ranging from very positive, such as love or strong friendships, to very negative, such as disdain or hate. These behaviors can be broadly subdivided into positivity, neutrality, and negativity. When the quantity of interactive behaviors is plotted against corresponding relationship values, a straight line is obtained, which can be called the line of interpretation or the behavior interpretation line (Figure 14). Each individual and group uses a particular line of interpretation to assign a meaning to observed conduct from other people. Individuals and groups also act toward others with intent to establish relationships based on their own cultures' interpretation line; therefore, every line of interpretation has a corresponding line of overt action or reaction (Figure 14). The degree of correlation between lines of interpretation and action relates to the individual's or group's ability to accurately understand behavior and reciprocate evenly based on the perceived relationship.

Depending on the degree of development, extent of competition for resources, historical background, geography, genetic predisposition, and multiple other factors, a person's or group's line of interpretation may be shifted from left to right along the horizontal (behavioral) axis, as illustrated in Figure 15. Cultures having separate lines of interpretation will assign different meanings to same behaviors. They will also express same relationships in different ways. Behavior that designates strong friendship in one culture may only mean politeness in another and something seen as neutral conduct in one society may elsewhere be taken as a sign of disdain or hate.

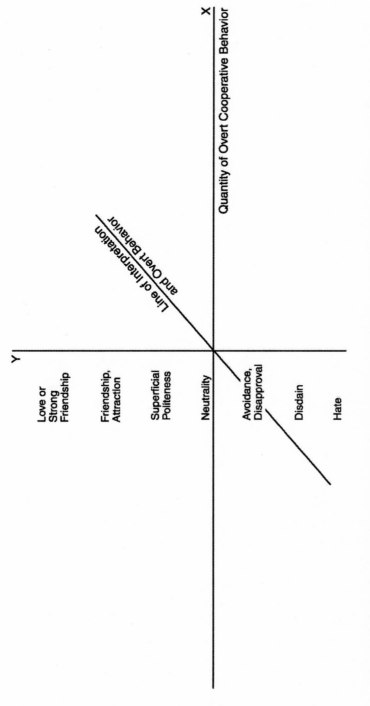

FIG. 14. Behavior interpretation and reciprocation are linear phenomena. With increasingly positive relationships, greater levels of cooperation take place between people and vice-versa: negative relationships will lead to progressively more negative actions in direct proportion to the hostility of relationship.

Michael Pak, M.D.

Variations in behavior interpretation follow a predictable pattern. In cultures with a left-shifted interpretation, small quantities of positive behavior have a large positive meaning, while large quantities of negative behavior have a relatively small negative meaning. Conversely, in cultures with a right-shifted interpretation, large quantities of positive behavior are assigned a small positive meaning, while small signs of negative behavior are seen as big hostility; therefore, right-shifted societies demand extensive cooperation to establish or maintain positive relationships. Here, only small quantities of negative behavior or even the absence of adequate cooperation can set up very negative relationships.

Miscommunication of behavior and dysfunctional reactions frequently result from contact between individuals and groups with different behavior interpretation lines.

People with left-shifted interpretations generally perceive right-shifted behavior as significantly more positive than it actually is, while people with right-shifted interpretations generally misunderstand left-shifted behavior as being significantly more hostile than it really is. This interpretational gap greatly contributes to cross-cultural misunderstandings, culture shock, and conflict.

Figure 15 demonstrates the variations in cultural interpretation of positive and negative behavior. In Culture A, which represents a person or society with a left-shifted interpretation line, absence of communication and cooperation represents the standard neutral behavior (both X and Y have zero value). In Culture C, which has the most right-shifted line of interpretation, absence of communication between people in the course of daily conduct signifies a very antagonistic relationship such as disdain or hate (zero X has a very large negative Y value). Culture B is an intermediate state in which absence of communication may have a moderate negative meaning such as disapproval. A person from Culture A may interact with Cultures B or C and ignore others or show minimal

94

positive signs such as brief eye contact and little or no verbal approval. While from the standpoint of left-shifted interpretation, this behavior has a neutral or somewhat positive meaning, in right-shifted cultures, it is understood as hostility and the person is misinterpreted as arrogant or even hateful. He or she risks retribution without ever meaning to start a conflict.

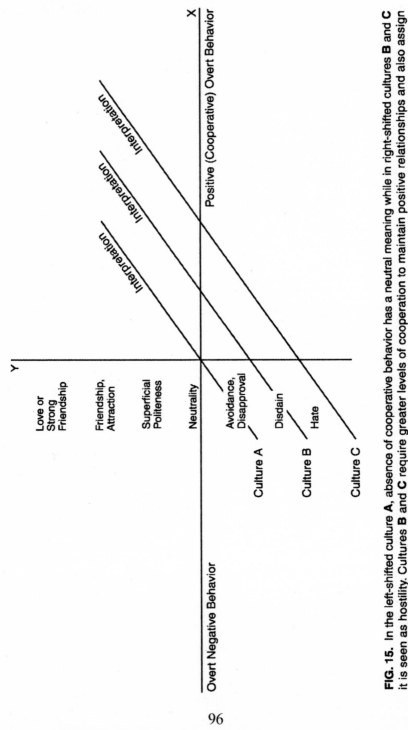

FIG. 15. In the left-shifted culture **A**, absence of cooperative behavior has a neutral meaning while in right-shifted cultures **B** and **C** it is seen as hostility. Cultures **B** and **C** require greater levels of cooperation to maintain positive relationships and also assign larger negative meanings to negative behaviors.

As an expression of mild negative meaning such as disapproval, people from left-shifted cultures may give out verbal or nonverbal reprimands. Examples include a frown, a spoken warning, raised voice, yelling, or even physical contact such as pushing or hitting. The quantity and intensity of this behavior depends on both the amount of negative meaning the behavior is intended to convey and the degree of a person's left shift. In communication with right-shifted cultures, this behavior may be perceived as having significantly more negative meaning, such as intense hate, in which case significant and/or prolonged negative overreaction is likely to occur. People from left-shifted cultures can be mistakenly perceived as being uninhibited, hateful or irrational. Conversely, if people from a right-shifted culture try to express disapproval or anger, they may only show an absence of communication. When interacting with a left-shifted culture their behavior may be seen as neutral conduct, in which case there is a failure to respond adequately or to respond at all.

On the behavior spectrum's more negative end, nonverbal and verbal warnings and threats coming form right-shifted individuals or groups, which represent very strong hostility, are seen by culturally left-shifted individuals and groups as having only mild negative meaning, which leads to failure to fully understand the magnitude of the warning and results in a significant underreaction.

Generally, along the entire spectrum, same negative behaviors involve comparatively greater negative emotions and meanings in right-shifted cultures than in left-shifted cultures. This expectation includes extreme forms of negative behavior, such as physical violence or homicide, which have more negative meanings and consequences, and involve more planning when performed in right-shifted cultures.

On the behavior spectrum's positive end, when friendship or attraction is expressed in left-shifted cultures, only small quantities of positive behavior are needed (only brief eye contact, a smile, or minimal cooperation may be adequate in this culture). In a right-shifted society, however, more extensive positive behavior is required, including prolonged periods of conversation and extensive cooperation.

A person from the left-shifted Culture A who is trying to express mild positive sentiments such as politeness may be misinterpreted by someone from a right-shifted culture as being indifferent or even avoidant. When communicating strongly positive intentions, the same person may be seen as being only formally polite. Along the entire length of behavior spectrum, the left-shifted person is seen as significantly less positive than he or she intends to be.

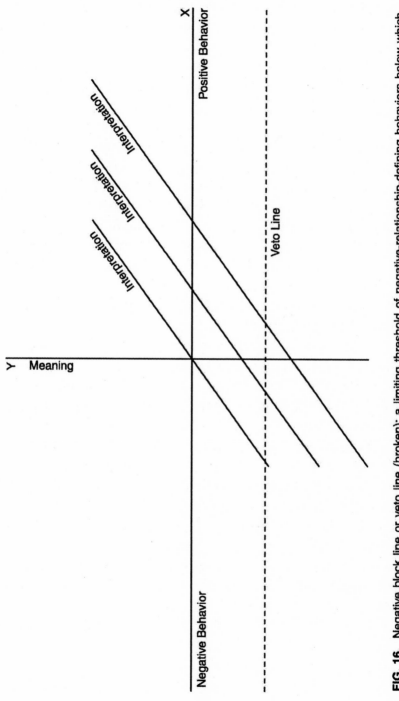

FIG. 16. Negative block line or veto line (broken): a limiting threshold of negative-relationship-defining behaviors below which there is a greatly increased probability of relationship breakdown.

Negative block can be defined as a prohibition of public display and direct expression of negative-relationship-defining behaviors. The expression "negative-relationship-defining behavior" is used rather than "negative behavior" because this category includes inadequate cooperation as well as actual negative behaviors. Figure 16 illustrates a hypothetical, horizontal negative block line or veto line, which is defined as a hypothetical limiting threshold below which there is a greatly increased probability of relationship breakdown or a state of anomie. Behaviors below this line can provoke immoderate negative responses, including multiple reactions disproportionate to the initial behavior and/or planning and performing a single action designed to eliminate the opposing person or group. Increasing right-shift results in a progressively lower threshold required to cross the veto line. Future research and observation will need to carefully examine the existence of such a threshold phenomenon.

With a cultural right shift, progressively greater hostility toward negative behaviors occurs and the society prohibits these actions as a part of direct or overt behavior. As a result, in right-shifted cultures, there is a decrease in relative proportion of negative behavior manifested in a direct, open manner and a relative increase in indirect and/or covert negative behavior. This phenomenon falls into the category of third-dimensional behavior and its magnitude is related to the Z-axis. Third-dimensional behavior can be defined as all negative and positive actions or reactions, individual or organized, which are conducted in an indirect and/or covert manner. The set of third-dimensional behaviors associated with a single line of interpretation can be called a line of indirect/covert action or reaction.

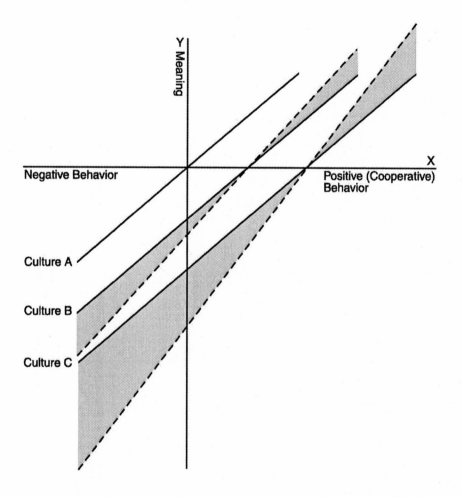

FIG. 17. With increasing cultural right shift, progressively greater quantities of both negative and positive behavior are displaced into the third dimension (along the **Z** axis) becoming indirect and/or covert (broken lines).

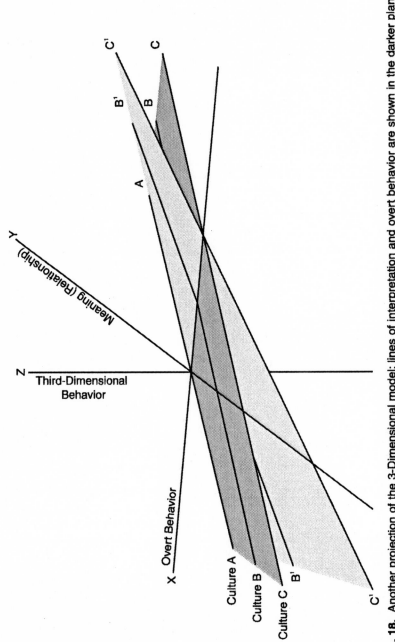

FIG. 18. Another projection of the 3-Dimensional model: lines of interpretation and overt behavior are shown in the darker plane (**A-B-C**) while lines of associated indirect/covert behavior are shown in the lighter plane (**B'-C'**).

In the course of a society's abandonment of its left-shifted culture and its acquisition of right-shifted interpretation and behavior patterns, one would expect a decrease in the incidence of all negative behaviors enacted openly or directly and a concomitant increase in planning and performance of indirect and covert behaviors. This expectation includes even extreme antagonistic actions, such as physical violence and homicide, which, in a left-shifted culture, are more likely to be a part of the second dimension (open and direct), while in a right-shifted culture, they become covert and indirect.

An example of a cross-cultural type of interaction that could lead to third-dimensional behavior would be a person from right-shifted Culture C who is being verbally threatened or physically assaulted by someone from left-shifted Culture A. In this situation, the level of hostility perceived is far greater than intended. The response may be immediate and direct, with its emotional intensity being much greater than the initial aggressive action. It may also be toned down in the immediate setting and followed by an extensive third-dimensional response. Subsequent reaction may include prosecution, private or public denunciation, planning of actions against the offending individual or group, etc., with the latter reactions being indirect and/or covert. The overall negative reaction is likely to be significantly greater than the initial provocation. By contrast, the expected response from a culturally left-shifted individual or group would more likely be direct and overt (verbal or physical aggression) and accompanied by comparatively less negative emotion and meaning. There would be little or no subsequent third-dimensional behavior.

A cultural right shift leads to a prohibition of public display of positive as well as negative relationships, which results in increasing quantities of cooperative behavior being displaced into the third dimension and performed covertly or indirectly. The magnitude is correlated to positive aspects of the Z-axis. Right-shifted cultures would, therefore, be marked by a decrease in public expression of friendship, affection, and cooperation and an increasingly private, covert, and/or indirect way of performing cooperation.

Increasing cultural right shift can be expected to lead to the development of extensive public and private institutions that allow for indirect or covert expression of positive emotions and relationships. It is also predicted to induce the development of secret organizations, groups, meetings, etc., which allow for positive relationships to be expressed in a clandestine manner.

As a rule, with an increasing cultural right shift, the spectrum of both positive and negative behaviors permitted to be done in a direct, open manner becomes progressively narrowed. There is a concomitant displacement of behaviors into the third dimension, beginning with the most extreme relationship-defining behaviors from each end. Extreme right shift, therefore, leads to a prohibition of direct expression and public display of all behaviors except for a very narrow range of those which designate the exact neutrality of relationship. Furthermore, with increasing right shift, progressively greater quantities of cooperative behavior are required to maintain neutral relationships.

Whether the elimination of behaviors from second dimension and their displacement into the third dimension is a purely a continuous phenomenon without a threshold (or whether thresholds exist, which would result in a step-like distributions) needs to be determined by future research and observation.

During any given time period, a particular population's collective set of relationships can be defined as a bell-shaped distribution along its cultural line of interpretation. By sampling the behavioral responses of a representative group in a particular society and knowing its line of interpretation, it could be possible to determine the predominant relationships that exist within it (positive, negative, or neutral). The three-dimensional model may be used to predict the probability and type of positive and negative events, including the most extreme behaviors, such as physical violence, homicide, and war. It could help to reduce the probability of these events by establishing methods to keep medians of population distributions within the safe ranges of Y-axis (positive and neutral). Geographic areas where variations exist can be identified and recommendations can be made to improve intergroup relations and prevention of dysfunctional interactions and conflicts caused by gaps between interpretation lines.

Scientific verification of a threshold phenomenon such as a negative block or veto threshold might show that relationship breakdowns and extreme negative behaviors are naturally occurring events in societies engaged in heavy competition over resources and help to prevent them.

The relationship between behavior interpretation modes and disease entities could be an area of great interest to public health. The incidence of conditions such as diabetes, heart disease, hypertension, and others may well be related to the forementioned behavior patterns. Examination of these relationships may provide new directions for development and expansion of medical research in the twenty-first century.

The three-dimensional model can establish a framework around which to build our understanding of interactive behavior, our actions, and thought process. It may provide a scientific basis for cultural relativism as well as develop avenues for future research in branches of science that deal with human interactions and society.